PHILIP ALLAN

LITERATURE GUIDE

Ë

Contents

Using this guide

Why read this guide?

The purposes of this A-level Literature Guide are to enable you to organise your thoughts and responses to the text, deepen your understanding of key features and aspects and help you to address the particular requirements of examination questions and coursework tasks in order to obtain the best possible grade. It will also prove useful to those of you writing a coursework piece on the text as it provides a number of summaries, lists, analyses and references to help with the content and construction of the assignment.

Note that teachers and examiners are seeking above all else evidence of an *informed personal response to the text*. A guide such as this can help you to understand the text and form your own opinions, and it can suggest areas to think about, but it cannot replace your own ideas and responses as an informed and autonomous reader.

Page references in this guide refer to the 2006 Penguin Classics edition of the novel, edited by Stevie Davies. This edition has an excellent introduction and comprehensive chapter notes, which are invaluable to students.

How to make the most of this guide

You may find it useful to read sections of this guide when you need them, rather than reading it from start to finish. For example, you may find it helpful to read the *Contexts* section before you start reading the text, or to read the *Chapter summaries and commentaries* section in conjunction with the text — whether to back up your first reading of it at school or college or to help you revise. The sections relating to the Assessment Objectives will be especially useful in the weeks leading up to the exam.

Philip Allan Updates, an imprint of Hodder Education, an Hachette UK company, Market Place, Deddington, Oxfordshire OX15 0SE

Orders

Bookpoint Ltd, 130 Milton Park, Abingdon, Oxfordshire OX14 4SB

tel: 01235 827827

fax: 01235 400401

e-mail: education@bookpoint.co.uk

Lines are open 9.00 a.m.–5.00 p.m., Monday to Saturday, with a 24-hour message answering service. You can also order through the Philip Allan Updates website: www.philipallan.co.uk

© Anne Crow 2010

ISBN 978-1-4441-1625-0

First printed 2010

Impression number 5 4

Year 2014 2013

Printed in Spain

P02130

Cover photo: Charlotte Gainsbourg as Jane Eyre in Franco Zeffirelli's 1996 film version of *Jane Eyre*. © Corbis Sygma

Key elements

Look at the **Context** boxes to find interesting facts that are relevant to the text.

| Context |

Be exam-ready

Broaden your thinking about the text by answering the questions in the **Pause for thought** boxes. These help you to consider your own opinions in order to develop your skills of criticism and analysis.

Pause for **Thought**

Build critical skills

Taking it further boxes suggest poems, films, etc. that provide further background or illuminating parallels to the text.

Taking it **Further** ➤

Where to find out more

Use the **Task** boxes to develop your understanding of the text and test your knowledge of it. Answers for some of the tasks are given online, and do not forget to look online for further self-tests on the text.

Task

Test yourself

Follow up cross references to the **Top ten quotations** (see pp. 90–93), where each quotation is accompanied by a commentary that shows why it is important.

❮ Top ten *quotation*

Know your text

Don't forget to go online: **www.philipallan.co.uk/literatureguidesonline** where you can find masses of additional resources **free**, including interactive questions, podcasts, exam answers and a glossary.

Synopsis

Brontë introduces us to ten-year-old Jane Eyre on the day she first rebels against injustice. She is an orphan being raised by her aunt, Mrs Reed, who resents her presence. One day, as punishment for fighting back against her bullying cousin, Jane's aunt locks Jane in the red-room, in which Jane's Uncle Reed died. Jane grows frightened, screams and faints. When she wakes, the apothecary listens to her unhappiness and suggests that Jane be sent away to school.

She is sent to Lowood Institution, a charity school under the management of Mr Brocklehurst, a cruel, hypocritical and abusive man. Brocklehurst preaches a doctrine of poverty and privation to his students, while his own family lives in luxury. At Lowood, Jane makes friends with Helen Burns, an inspirational girl who teaches Jane endurance and self-denial. A typhus epidemic kills many of the poorly nourished girls, and Helen dies of consumption. The epidemic attracts attention to the unhealthy conditions at Lowood and this results in the removal of Brocklehurst as manager; after this Jane's life improves dramatically. She is happy at Lowood, largely due to the good influence of Miss Temple, the superintendent, and she spends eight more years there, six as a student and two as a teacher.

When Miss Temple leaves to get married, Jane is restless and yearns for new experiences. She accepts a governess position at Thornfield, where she teaches a pretty French girl named Adèle. Mrs Fairfax, the housekeeper, is in charge of the house, but Jane's employer is a gruff, moody man named Edward Rochester, in whose company Jane finds particular delight. Jane sometimes hears strange noises from the upper floors and one night she saves Rochester from a fire; Jane does not believe his explanation of these strange happenings. Rochester brings home a party of guests, including the beautiful Blanche Ingram, and Jane struggles against jealousy and despair. Rochester leads everyone to expect that he will propose to Blanche but, surprisingly, he proposes to Jane, who accepts almost disbelievingly.

In the church, a solicitor halts the wedding ceremony, claiming that Rochester is already married. Richard Mason testifies that his sister, Bertha, whom Rochester married years before in Jamaica, is still alive. Rochester takes everyone back to Thornfield to view his wife, who is imprisoned in the attic and guarded by Grace Poole. Jane retreats to her room and prays, emerging some hours later to find Rochester waiting for her. He tries to persuade her to stay but that night she slips away and takes the coach to an unknown distant place.

When her money runs out, Jane is comforted by nature but she becomes faint through lack of food. Eventually, she wanders to the isolated Moor House at Marsh End, sees two friendly ladies through the window and begs for shelter. She is turned away by the servant and collapses, but St John Rivers, the clergyman and brother to the ladies, arrives and rescues her. For three days Jane lies ill, then she lives happily with Diana and Mary Rivers until they have to return to their positions as governesses. St John finds Jane a job teaching at a village school in Morton. He surprises her one day by declaring that her uncle, John Eyre, has died and left her a large fortune. When Jane asks how he received this news, he shocks her further by declaring that John Eyre was also his uncle. Delighted to have found a family, Jane immediately decides to share her inheritance equally with her three cousins.

St John plans to travel to India as a missionary and urges Jane to accompany him as his wife. Jane refuses, but St John pressures her, and she nearly gives in. At his third proposal, she prays and then hears Rochester's voice calling her. She hurries back to Thornfield to find that it has been burned to the ground. Rochester saved the servants and returned for his wife, who had started the fire, but she threw herself off the battlements. Rochester lost his eyesight and one of his hands. Jane travels on to Rochester's new residence, Ferndean.

At Ferndean, Rochester and Jane rebuild their relationship and soon marry. At the end of her story, Jane writes that she has been married for ten blissful years. After two years of blindness, Rochester regained the sight of one eye and was able to see their first son at his birth. Jane learns in a letter that St John is expecting to die in India, but she is filled with admiration for him.

Chapter summaries and commentaries

Chapter I

Brontë starts Jane's fictional autobiography with the first time she rebels against injustice and male oppression, fighting back when John Reed bullies her. From the beginning Jane is established as an outsider, excluded from the Reed family group.

Commentary: **As the novel opens, the weather is cold and forbidding, reflecting the coldness and loneliness of Jane's world. Brontë juxtaposes the outside scene with a warm family scene at the fireside, from which Jane is excluded. Jane is resented by the family as a poor relation foisted on them by Mr Reed, who seems to remain the head of the household even after his death. They humble her with a consciousness of her physical and social inferiority. The view from the window seat reflects Jane's own misery and is obscured by mist. This metaphorically suggests that she cannot see beyond her own unhappiness, and that her future is also obscured. However, just as the mist outside will lift, so her future will emerge more clearly, and Brontë has opened the story at the point when her life is about to change. Until this point, Jane has been unhappy, but there has been no dramatic focus to interest readers. Jane's ambiguous social standing sets up most of the novel's internal tension and conflict, and Jane's struggle against male oppression begins with John Reed.**

Jane finds refuge in the inner world of her imagination, interpreting the stories told by the vignettes in Bewick's *History of British Birds*. In one picture, for instance, she sees two becalmed ships as 'phantoms', and she passes quickly over 'the fiend pinning down the thief's pack behind him' and 'the black, horned thing seated aloof on a rock, surveying a distant crowd surrounding a gallows'. These pictures give a sense of foreboding and foreshadow the events to come, introducing elements of the Gothic genre. Brontë draws on this isolation, the

Context

Thomas Bewick (1753–1828) was an English wood engraver and ornithologist.

Taking it
Further

Study the vignettes from Bewick's *History of British Birds* in the downloads of resources at www.philipallan.co.uk/literatureguidesonline

association with death (the wreck, the churchyard and the gallows), the workings of the supernatural (the ghastly moon, the phantoms and the fiend), as well as the presence of some undefined evil, in other contexts throughout the novel.

Two of Bewick's vignettes that caught Jane's imagination, the becalmed ships and the thief with the pack

From her greater maturity, the adult Jane guides the reader to be aware of the limited perceptions of the child. As little Jane looks at the pictures of birds in 'forlorn regions of dreary space', she tells us that the pictures acted as a stimulus for her imagination, but that this was 'shadowy, like all the half-comprehended notions that float dim through children's brains'. Brontë establishes them as formative influences on Jane's as yet 'undeveloped understanding and imperfect feelings'.

Jane is a passionate character with a vivid imagination, so she might not be an entirely reliable narrator. Her memories may be highly coloured and her desire to present her story as a Cinderella-style fairy tale may lead her to exaggerate.

Chapter II

Jane is locked in the red-room, where Mr Reed died, as punishment for her behaviour. She grows frightened and screams but is locked in again. She loses consciousness.

Commentary: **Jane's position in the household is confusing. She is a member of the family but she is a poor relation and therefore John is her 'young master', and she is totally dependent on the Reeds' charity. She is resented by the servants as 'less than a servant, for you do nothing for your keep'. The difference is that whereas '[t]hey will have a great deal of money...you will have none'. The irony is that John will dissipate their fortune whereas Jane will inherit her uncle's wealth.**

The threat to bind Jane to a chair is one of a number of hints Brontë gives us that there is some comparison or parallel to be

TASK 1

Write Mrs Reed's account of the incident of the red-room. Try to build upon Brontë's presentation of her character and echo specific aspects of her form, structure and language. Write a brief commentary to accompany your new text, explaining how and where you have tried to reflect the original novel.

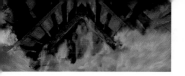

drawn between Jane and Bertha. While Jane is behaving 'like a mad cat', locking her up in solitary confinement does not teach her to behave in the manner expected of her; it induces a temporary madness in the form of a fit.

Like all the other houses in this book, except Ferndean, this house is apparently run by women but, in reality, Mr Reed still dominates the household from the grave. Mrs Reed keeps Jane only because of 'a hard-wrung pledge' to her husband on his death-bed. The room in which he died is kept virtually untouched, like a shrine. The reason for Jane's imprisonment is her rebellion against the domination of the male member of the family, waiting to take his father's place. The women in the house uphold this system of patriarchy, supporting the concept of male dominance and power.

Apart from the 'snowy' white bed and chair, which enhance the religious imagery, the room is, as its name states, red. Like the window seat where she sought refuge, the red-room has folds of scarlet drapery and is an enclosed space that symbolises Jane's private, internal world, but here she is trapped and vulnerable to her overactive imagination. Such excess of redness suggests passion and, indeed, sexuality; Jane is ten, approaching puberty, so perhaps Brontë intends this episode to be seen as a kind of rite of passage, a time when she must put childhood behind her.

Brontë carefully builds up the child's growing sense of terror. The bed linen 'glared' comfortlessly white, and the atmosphere was 'chill', 'silent', 'remote', 'lonely', even the dust was 'quiet'. The list of the contents of the secret drawer builds up to the portrait of the deceased husband, which Jane describes as the 'spell'. Under this spell, Jane sees the bed as a 'tabernacle' (the curtained tent that housed the Jewish Ark of the Covenant), the curtains as 'shrouds', the chair as a 'throne', empty, but still symbolic of the ruler of this household. So, even after nine years, he still rules the house and, symbolically, even Jane's inner consciousness. Even her own reflection in the mirror is transformed into a 'strange' but fascinating figure with 'glittering' eyes, which reminds her of 'the tiny phantoms' that featured in Bessie's stories.

'Superstition' was taking hold of Jane's imagination, 'but it was not yet her hour for complete victory'. This personification shows how the child was at the mercy of things beyond her control. The tension eased somewhat as Jane remembered her grievances, and, in another personification, 'Resolve' instigated thoughts of

Context

In the Bible, the Ark of the Covenant is a vessel containing the tablets of stone inscribed with the Ten Commandments.

TASK 2

At what other key moment does Jane see a strange figure in her mirror, and become 'insensible from terror'? Consider how Brontë uses mirrors as symbols.

running away or starving herself to death. The tension gradually builds again as she listens to the beating rain and the howling wind and realises that, if she succeeds, she will be put in the vault under the church. This reminds her that, according to superstition, spirits are supposed to revisit 'the earth to punish the perjured and avenge the oppressed'.

Brontë has shown how Jane's mind has been prepared for horror and her nerves shaken by agitation, so, fearing that Mr Reed's ghost was coming to comfort her, she interprets a strange moving light as 'a herald of some coming vision from another world'. Her growing terror is conveyed in the short, abrupt, monosyllabic clauses: 'My heart beat thick, my head grew hot; a sound filled my ears'; her absolute panic in the breathless syntax of 'something seemed near me; I was oppressed, suffocated: endurance broke down'.

As a mature woman, Jane Rochester still feels the pain of rejection and the anger at the injustice, but she has learned to temper this with understanding, although the words she chooses suggest that she has not forgiven. Four times she refers to the young Jane as a 'thing' when she is explaining why she was an outsider at Gateshead Hall. This non-human epithet suggests that, at the time of writing, she is still indignant that they could not treat her like a human being with feelings and emotional needs. However, with hindsight, she now understands that her aunt saw her as 'a compound of virulent passions, mean spirit, and dangerous duplicity'.

Chapter III

Jane wakes in the nursery, where the apothecary has been called to treat her. She tells her story for the first time when she explains to Mr Lloyd why she is miserable. He suggests that she might like to go to school.

Commentary: **Jane wakes to 'a terrible red glare, crossed with thick black bars'; it took her five minutes to recognise this as the nursery fire; this is a powerful image of how the safety of childhood has turned into a vivid image of confined passion.**

Gulliver's Travels **is a popular, but very dark, satire by Jonathan Swift, the first two books of which can be read as children's stories about pygmies and giants. Brontë marks the start of Jane's growth to maturity by showing her changed perception of a book that had been a source of delight but is now full of dread and desolation.**

Context

Jonathan Swift (1667–1745) was a satirist, essayist, political writer, poet and cleric of Anglo-Irish origin.

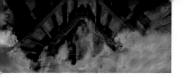

Bessie sings an unknown ballad, probably written by Brontë, that foreshadows what will happen to Jane when she is lost and alone on the moors, and which sums up an important theme of the novel — the search for a home. Significantly, the popular view of God is that he is a 'friend to the poor orphan child'.

Brontë has introduced Guy Fawkes, the notorious Catholic conspirator, because of his association with fire and explosiveness. The adult Jane seems amused that Miss Abbott thought of her as a dangerous anarchist.

Context

Guy Fawkes (1570–1606) was part of a Catholic group who plotted to blow up the Houses of Parliament on 5 November 1605. By killing King James I and the members of his parliament, the group hoped to end Protestant rule and its discrimination against Catholics.

Chapter IV

Mr Brocklehurst comes to inspect Jane, and his hypocritical account of Lowood Institution reveals that it is designed to prepare the daughters of impoverished gentlemen for their subservient position in society. Jane is hurt when Mrs Reed tells him she is deceitful and, after he has left, accuses her fiercely of injustice and cruelty.

Commentary: **Jane has a strongly developed sense of justice and of her own worth, in spite of the Reed family's attempts to humble her. She also has a strong need to love and be loved, and she lavishes her thwarted love on a doll. In this chapter Jane has learned to stand up for herself but, although she is triumphant at her victory, vengeance leaves a sour taste.**

Chapter V

Jane leaves Gateshead for Lowood, where the poor food, harsh discipline and inadequate uniforms are all designed to prevent the girls from blossoming into young women. The emphasis on religion hypocritically implies that their suffering is for the good of their souls. Jane meets Helen Burns, who explains about the supposedly 'charitable' institution.

Commentary: **The irony of the inscription lauding Mrs Brocklehurst's 'good works' is underlined by the sound of Helen's cough; she will soon die from the tuberculosis that the privations at Lowood have done much to exacerbate.**

Chapter VI

Jane observes Helen being victimised again, even though she is the only girl in the class who can answer Miss Scatcherd's questions. Jane feels impotent anger but Helen reveals no emotion. Helen tries to teach her the New Testament values of endurance and forgiveness. Jane tells Helen the tale of her sufferings. Helen explains her belief that eternity is 'a rest — a mighty home, not a terror and an abyss'.

Commentary: **Through the lesson on Charles I, with questions on 'tonnage', 'poundage' and 'ship-money', illegal taxes that led to the English Civil War and the king's execution by parliament, Brontë raises the question of whether rebellion is ever justifiable.**

Chapter VII

Brocklehurst inspects the school and explains his policies to reject what is natural as dangerous and bad; nature is to be crushed as part of the girls' training. He declares Jane to be a liar and humiliates her in front of the school, but Helen gives her an inspirational look.

Commentary: **Ironically, the regime at Lowood does not foster Christian values but promotes bullying, as the bigger girls hog the fire and steal food from the younger girls. Brontë's choice of the 'fifth, sixth and seventh chapters of St Matthew' is ironic as they contain the Sermon on the Mount, which is mostly concerned with the promise of reward in heaven for those who have suffered on earth. Brocklehurst believes in predestination and tells everyone that Jane is a 'castaway', meaning that she is beyond salvation, already claimed by the devil.**

Chapter VIII

After her ordeal, Jane wishes to die because of the humiliation. Helen reassures her, and Miss Temple invites them both to her room, where Jane tells Miss Temple her story in a restrained manner. The superintendent writes for confirmation to Mr Lloyd. Jane's name is publicly cleared; she works hard and is promoted to a higher class.

Commentary: **This is a significant moment in Jane's development, as she has learned to arrange her story coherently.**

Chapter IX

As Jane flourishes at Lowood, the weather improves and she is given more freedom. However, the reason for this is that there is a serious outbreak of typhus and many of the girls die. Jane suddenly realises that Helen, who has consumption (tuberculosis), is very ill and she is determined to see her. Helen is looking forward to death as a blessed release from suffering, but Jane questions whether heaven exists.

Commentary: **On p. 94, Brontë repeats the same point: 'it entered my mind as it had never done before'; 'my mind made its first**

Context

King Charles I (1600–49): in a power struggle with parliament, Charles demanded money by right of what he believed was his divine status as king. Many people opposed him, objecting in particular to the taxes he imposed without parliamentary consent. His actions led to the Civil War and his execution.

Context

Mr Brocklehurst is a Calvinist. A distinctive issue in Calvinist theology is its doctrine of salvation, which holds that humans cannot influence the process of salvation, and that only God is responsible for it. Salvation is therefore not the achievement of the one who is saved, but a new work of creation by God.

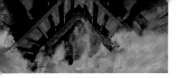

earnest effort'; 'for the first time'; 'for the first time'. This emphasises that it is an important turning point for Jane, when she begins to understand the meaning of death.

'Resurgam' is Latin for 'I shall rise again.' The word encapsulates Helen's belief in heaven and a benevolent God.

Chapter X

Context

At the time of publication, Brontë's critics were outraged, because Victorian women were not supposed to extend their horizons beyond home and duty.

Jane Rochester summarises the eight years following Helen's death. The outbreak of typhus led to an enquiry and the school was reformed. Jane works hard, gaining an excellent education, and eventually becomes a teacher. When Miss Temple leaves to get married, Lowood no longer feels like home. Jane is restless, so she advertises for and accepts a position as governess. Bessie visits her, declares that she looks like a lady, and tells her about a visit from Jane's uncle seven years earlier.

Commentary: **The blue peaks on the horizon, which Jane longs to surmount, symbolise her aspirations.**

Chapter XI

Jane arrives at Thornfield late at night and her apprehensions are dispelled by a warm welcome from Mrs Fairfax. Next day she meets Adèle and learns about the absent master of the house. She is shown round the house; the possibility of some horrible secret, aroused by a tragic and preternatural laugh, is dispelled by the appearance of Grace Poole.

Context

'Bluebeard', published in 1697 by the French writer Charles Perrault, is a folktale about one in a series of wives of a murderous French nobleman. She tries to avoid meeting the same grisly fate as her predecessors.

Commentary: **There is irony in Jane's wordplay on the name of the house: 'My couch had no thorns in it that night.'**

Like the red-room at Gateshead, Rochester's drawing room is 'furnished with a general blending of snow and fire', so Brontë reminds us of past terrors and hints at terrors to come.

In the fairy story, Bluebeard allows his young wife to open any door she likes, except one. Curious, she enters the forbidden room and finds the bodies of his previous wives. Jane has been reading Gothic horror novels and is looking for adventure.

Chapter XII

Context

The Gytrash, a ghostly black dog legendary in northern England, is said to lie in wait for travellers on deserted roads.

After three pleasant months at Thornfield, Jane is restless. On the way to post a letter, she stops to watch a dramatic sunset. Hearing the clatter of hooves, she remembers Bessie's stories about the Gytrash, but the illusion is dispelled when a man appears on a horse and falls when the horse slips on the ice. Having helped him to remount, she is left feeling disturbed, unwilling to return to the 'fetters' of the unchanging pleasantness of her life. She recognises Rochester's dog on her return.

Commentary: **Brontë politicises women's rights, placing Jane's claim for equality with men in the context of 'political rebellions', revealing a strong awareness of the unrest among working people. This was thought very dangerous by some contemporary reviewers. Her use of the electrical image 'earth' suggests that this silent revolt is potentially explosive.**

Chapter XIII

The following evening, Jane and Adèle are invited to join Rochester. Jane studies his features by the light of the fire, observing the qualities of decisiveness and a hasty temper. He interrogates her about her time at Lowood, scrutinises three of her paintings and then dismisses her abruptly. Mrs Fairfax gives Jane a brief and incomplete summary of Rochester's troubles.

Commentary: **In the first of many such references, Rochester links Jane with the spirit world, accusing her of bewitching his horse and spreading ice on the causeway. When he questions her about her relatives Jane answers evasively: 'none that I ever saw'. Misleading him like this encourages him later to ask her to marry him, thinking she has no relatives to interfere.**

The first painting owes its setting to Bewick's *History of British Birds*, but it has been painted in the style of John Martin, and the subject is reminiscent of his *Assuaging the Waters*. Perhaps the black cormorant proudly displaying the bracelet was subconsciously suggested by Brocklehurst, who let the girls suffer and die, while his own family appeared richly dressed. In Milton's *Paradise Lost*, the cormorant is a symbol of temptation and deception, 'devising death/To them who lived'. We recall the image of the drowned girl when Jane quotes from the Psalms at the end of Chapter XXVI. The second painting depicts the mountain of Latmos, where, according to Greek mythology, Selene, Goddess of the Moon, first saw and fell in love with Endymion, vowing to protect him for evermore. The Evening Star is the planet Venus, goddess of love. The third painting also owes its setting to Bewick. 'The likeness of a kingly crown' and 'the shape which shape had none' are quotations from *Paradise Lost* and they refer to Death, who is one of the keepers guarding the gates of hell, preventing Satan and the other fallen angels from leaving.

*Pause for **Thought***

What do we learn from the pictures Jane painted at Lowood about her inner feelings at that time? How does Brontë use the paintings to foreshadow later scenes in the novel?

Context

John Martin (1789–1854) was a popular nineteenth-century English Romantic painter. A print of *Belshazzar's Feast* hung on the parlour wall of the Haworth vicarage, where Brontë grew up.

Context

Paradise Lost, an epic poem by the seventeenth-century poet John Milton, concerns the Christian story of the fall of man.

Chapter XIV

Some days later, Jane and Adèle are summoned again. Rochester tries to bully Jane but she proves a match for him and he clearly admires this. He recognises the restlessness in Jane's nature.

Commentary: **Jane's narrative is unreliable when she interprets Rochester's smile and sparkling eyes as evidence that he has been drinking, whereas we realise that he is animated by her presence. Brontë poignantly uses the past tense as Jane Rochester writes: 'he had great, dark eyes'.**

Through Rochester's words, Brontë reveals that, like Byron's heroes, his present personality has been shaped by past events. He blames others for what he has become and regrets the path he took. Ironically, he tells Jane to 'Dread remorse when you are tempted to err'; it will be he who tempts her to 'err'. Brontë raises suspense by hinting at an insurmountable problem, and when he declares 'I have a right to get pleasure out of life: and I *will* get it, cost what it may', Brontë suggests that this is the point at which he decides that he will try to make Jane fall in love with him.

Chapter XV

Rochester tells Jane about his liaison with Céline Varens, Adèle's mother. The reader realises that Jane is falling in love with him. That night she hears strange noises, finds his bed on fire and douses the flames. Brontë hints that Rochester is also in love with Jane.

Commentary: **In the final paragraph, Brontë is referring to Bunyan's *The Pilgrim's Progress* where Beulah is the pleasant land beyond the Valley of the Shadow of Death. 'Beulah' in Hebrew means married. However, 'even in fancy' Jane is unable to reach it: 'Sense would resist delirium: judgment would warn passion.' Thus Brontë foreshadows later events.**

Chapter XVI

Rochester departs suddenly. Jane is flushed and feverish. Jane suspects Grace Poole of starting the fire and of having some secret hold over him. Grace Poole warns her to lock her door at night. Mrs Fairfax tells Jane about Blanche Ingram and Jane suspects that Rochester is planning to marry her. She warns herself of the danger of letting a secret love kindle within her.

*Pause for **Thought***

In a first-person narrative, it is difficult for the writer to give the inner feelings of other characters. How does Brontë use language and form to suggest Rochester's thoughts, while still preserving the mystery?

Context

Lord Byron (1788–1824) was a British poet and leading figure in Romanticism, whose reputation rests on his writings and his scandalous lifestyle. A popular but controversial figure in London society, he was also a revolutionary and later fought in the Greek War of Independence.

Commentary: **Jane's chosen medium is art rather than writing, so she spends two weeks painting a fine imaginary portrait of Blanche on ivory and sketches her own portrait quickly in crayons to persuade herself that Rochester will never fall in love with her. In her choice of media and the care she takes over the execution of the two portraits, she has emphasised the contrast between herself and her rival, vainly attempting to ensure that she will not fall victim to the 'madness' of a 'secret love'.**

Chapter XVII

Rochester writes that he is inviting guests, so extra servants are brought in and the house prepared. Gossiping servants fall silent as Jane approaches. The guests arrive; Jane's presence is required after dinner. She secretes herself in the window seat, from where she observes the guests, and the entrance of Rochester. She notes: 'He made me love him without looking at me.' Rochester encourages his guests to speak disparagingly about governesses. He sings a Corsair song, accompanied by Blanche, and Jane slips out. He follows her and insists that she attends every evening.

Commentary: **Jane's narrative is unreliable when she blames the coffee for the 'fiery glow' that suddenly rises to her face when Rochester's letter arrives. With the house party, Brontë takes advantage of Jane's ambivalent position to have her present but not included, so that she can give a satirical portrayal of the upper-class guests. As the gentlemen enter, Brontë reverts to the present tense so that we can feel Jane's spontaneous reactions to Rochester's arrival. This is the first time she has seen Rochester since the fire in his bedroom and this technique gives the episode more emotional intensity and dramatic impact. Lord Byron's Corsair is one of the Byronic heroes that influenced Brontë in her presentation of Rochester.**

> **Context**
>
> Corsairs were French ship owners paid by the government to attack enemy ships in wartime. The corsairs had a romantic reputation for being glamorous and swashbuckling. Byron's *The Corsair* (1814) sold 10,000 copies on the first day of publication.

Chapter XVIII

The house party has a game of charades; Jane is convinced that Rochester will marry Blanche. Later, Rochester departs on business and a stranger, Mr Mason, calls. A gypsy woman appears and insists on telling the fortunes of the young, single ladies.

Commentary: **Rochester's first role is as Blanche's bridegroom, a role presumably designed to arouse Jane's jealousy, but one that foreshadows the mock marriage he will put Jane through. In his second role, he is dressed as an Eastern emir, foreshadowing**

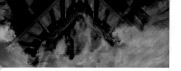

the way Jane feels that he behaves towards her during their engagement, like a sultan to a favoured slave. Brontë offers an unfavourable comment on the way he plays with Blanche's hopes by casting them as Eliezer tempting Rebecca to marry Isaac by proffering jewels. In the third role he is dressed as a desperate prisoner in Bridewell. This suggests his marital status, chained to a mad wife, and foreshadows Jane's first view of him at Ferndean, when she describes him as like 'some wronged and fettered wild beast or bird'.

Jane's self-restraint is put to the test at the prospect of Rochester marrying Blanche Ingram; she speaks metaphorically of her struggle with 'two tigers — jealousy and despair'.

The guests praise Mason's appearance, but Jane is repelled by him, describing him in a series of negatives: his eye had 'no meaning in its wandering', there was 'no power...no firmness... no thought...no command...'.

Chapter XIX

Through dressing as a gypsy, Rochester is able to read Jane's face by the light of the fire, confirming that she is passionate but will not give in to her feelings if they go against her conscience. He tries to lead Jane to reveal her feelings but she is guarded in her replies. When he drops his disguise, she tells him of Mason's arrival. He grips her hand convulsively and staggers, leaning on her for support.

Commentary: **After the charades, Rochester assumes yet another role. Appearances can be deceptive and we are invited to wonder whether the Rochester Jane thinks she knows is yet another disguise. In this scene, Brontë preserves the mystery by letting us view the scene as it was played out, without Jane Rochester's subsequent knowledge. This way she can keep the gypsy's identity secret, until Jane Eyre realises who the 'woman' really is. Jane preserves the visitor's anonymity by using various epithets to create an appropriately mysterious atmosphere. When Rochester dresses up as a 'gypsy', he knowingly takes on a persona that his guests will fear, not just for supposed psychic powers, but also because he threatens the harmony of the house, symbolised in the darkness of his appearance and the room. Jane also refers to him as 'sybil' (Chapter XVIII), a 'crone' (originally an old useless ewe but later used as a word for a withered old woman) and a 'strange being'.**

Brontë's narrative technique brings the scene alive, as if it is being played out in front of us rather than narrated from a distance of some eleven years. Most of this chapter is dialogue, with very little input by the narrator, except to act as stage directions. The fire is at the centre of this stage set. Rochester has extinguished the candle to aid his disguise and he is bending over the fire, which provides the only light in the room. He positions himself carefully so that his face is in shadow but Jane's illuminated, as he makes her kneel by the fire and look up while he examines her face. Jane complains that 'the fire scorches me'; Brontë uses the image of flames to represent sexual desire and, symbolically, Jane retreats from it as something dangerous. Previously, when Brontë used this fire imagery and Rochester's bed was aflame, it was Jane who doused the flames. Rochester recognises the passion within Jane but he does not know how to release it.

Brontë juxtaposes Rochester's decision to ask Jane to marry him with the appearance of Mason. Because Rochester hears of Bertha's brother's arrival precisely as he decides to commit bigamy, it gives him a blow that makes him stagger. However, the reader sees only his dramatic reaction and, like Jane, does not know the reason. For the second time, he has to lean on Jane's shoulder, which foreshadows the final section of the novel.

Jane lets her guard down when the 'gypsy' speaks of Rochester's gratitude at Blanche's attentions but Jane Rochester does not admit to allowing jealousy to cloud her judgement. She claims that the 'gypsy' wielded an almost magical power over her, and that she was 'involved in a web of mystification'. This scene adds to the Gothic tone of the novel, as well as creating more mystery as to the reason for Rochester's desperate fear of Mason.

It could be that Brontë has another motive in dressing her hero up as a woman. Possibly she is questioning the traditional male and female roles, exploring Rochester's dependence on Jane, even when he thinks he is in control, and anticipating the future at Ferndean.

Brontë employs two pseudo-sciences that were popular at the time when Rochester tries to establish Jane's character. 'Physiognomy' is interpreting the signs of the face, and 'phrenology' is interpreting the signs of the skull, because various parts of the head were thought to be responsible for

*TASK **3***

At what other points in the novel does Jane blame an external force for casting a sort of spell on her, rather than admit to her own weakness?

Context

Gothic — a medieval style of architecture that was revived in the late eighteenth century as a literary genre containing violence, death, horror, the supernatural and the macabre. Its settings are eerie ancient buildings, such as castles, during darkness and bad weather.

*TASK **4***

Find other places in the novel where Brontë makes use of physiognomy and phrenology.

Write Rochester's account of his evening disguised as a gypsy. Try to build upon Brontë's presentation of his character and echo specific aspects of her form, structure and language. Write a brief commentary to accompany your new text, explaining how and where you have tried to reflect the original novel.

Jane and Rochester on the stairs (Joan Fontaine and Orson Welles in the 1944 film)

different personal qualities. Brontë herself went to a phrenologist to have her skull read.

When Jane realises the 'gypsy's' true identity, four short questions convey her confusion. Her concern is that she may have revealed her inner feelings. However, ironically, it is to Rochester, not the 'gypsy', that she admits 'I'd give my life to serve you.'

Chapter XX

The moon wakes Jane, who hears a horrifying scream, followed by a struggle and cries for help. She observes the guests' consternation, dresses herself and waits in her room. The guests pacified, Rochester asks Jane to follow him to the third storey, where Mason lies bleeding. Rochester forbids them to speak and leaves Jane as nurse while he goes for the doctor. As dawn approaches, they return, and the doctor finds that Mason has been bitten and stabbed. The doctor and Mason depart. Rochester and Jane talk as the sun rises. The mystery deepens as he gives more hints about his past and talks of reformation through a stranger. Jane promises to obey him 'in all that is right'. He suddenly starts talking of marriage to Blanche.

Commentary: **Mason says 'She sucked my blood': Bertha is associated with a vampire, a re-animated corpse that feeds on the blood of the living. However, he also says, 'she said she'd drain my heart', so she is not merely reacting like a vampire or wild animal.**

Chapter XXI

Jane dreams of a baby and fears it is an ill omen. Her cousin John has squandered the family fortune and eventually committed suicide. Her dying Aunt Reed summons her to Gateshead to give Jane a three-year old letter from her uncle, John Eyre of Madeira. Mrs Reed had told him that Jane had died at Lowood.

Commentary: **Brontë often uses Jane's sensitivity to presentiments and signs to foreshadow coming events and create suspense.**

Jane has matured from the child who declared that she would never forgive her aunt. Significantly, Jane thinks of Helen Burns

and 'her faith — her doctrine of the equality of disembodied souls', the third-person determiner admitting that she does not believe it herself.

Jane briefly describes the vignettes she draws to pass the time. Two of them suggest the illustrations in Bewick's *History of British Birds*; perhaps we could read into the images of sea and a ship a wish to travel, to broaden her horizons. The other two are romantic images woven out of observation and imagination. No longer is she haunted by images of death and desolation, and the supernatural images are neither sinister nor despairing, but rather innocent and childlike. After this she draws the outline of a face, and her 'fingers proceeded actively to fill it with features', as if acting subconsciously, rather than under her direction. Once the portrait of Rochester is completed, she declares 'There, I had a friend's face under my gaze.' It seems that it is Rochester who has dispelled the loneliness and longing that inspired her early paintings.

Mrs Reed addresses Jane with the second person pronoun 'you' and then changes to the third person as she talks to herself about Jane: 'I had better tell her.' This suggests a distancing through shame. After Jane reads the letter, Mrs Reed reverts to the second person. It is ironic that Mrs Reed accused Jane of lying and now dies troubled by the lie she told Mr Eyre of Madeira.

Chapter XXII

After a month away, Jane returns to Thornfield. Mrs Fairfax has written to her of preparations for Rochester's wedding. She arrives at sunset and meets Rochester en route. He teases her and she admits to him that 'wherever you are is my home — my only home'.

Commentary: **Brontë suggests that Jane is ashamed of her weakness because she rejects responsibility for her admission, saying 'a force turned me round. I said — or something in me said for me, and in spite of me —'.**

Chapter XXIII

Jane meets Rochester in the orchard on Midsummer's Eve. He goads her into a declaration of her feelings and an assertion of her independence. Under the chestnut tree, he asks her to marry him. When she can be persuaded of his sincerity, she agrees. Rochester defies God and man; the weather changes suddenly, and lightning strikes the tree.

Context

Brontë defied nineteenth-century convention and outraged some critics by having Jane declare her passionate feelings for a man, especially one who is her social superior.

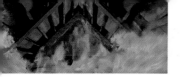

Commentary: **For an analysis of the beginning of this chapter see the 'Extended commentaries' in the *Working with the text* section. See the section on 'Symbolism' under *Form, structure and language* for an analysis of the chestnut-tree (p. 46 of this guide).**

'I have her, and will hold her': Rochester's choice of verbs reveals that he thinks of Jane as a possession.

Chapter XXIV

The next day, Rochester declares they will be married in four weeks; Jane feels both joy and fear. Mrs Fairfax warns Jane to be on her guard. While shopping she feels degraded by his attempts to buy her extravagant gifts, so she writes to her uncle in the hopes of a small independency. She keeps Rochester at arm's length by teasing him during their courtship.

Commentary: **When Rochester says 'wherever I stamped my hoof', he implies that, when he travelled in Europe, he was like a satyr, with the upper half of a man and the lower half of a goat. In classical mythology, satyrs were highly-sexed lovers of wine and women, ready for every physical pleasure. He sees her as a 'sylph', a spirit of the air, who will cleanse him of his sins. Ironically, Rochester himself destroys his hopes of a bigamous marriage; it is because he treats Jane like a possession that she writes to her uncle in Madeira in the hope of gaining financial independence.**

After the song, Brontë uses the third person pronoun 'he', even though their conversation is reported in quotation marks. This has the effect of distancing us from the conversation, which is an example of the way in which Jane kept him at a distance.

Context

Brontë wrote the song Rochester sings, inspired by her love for M Heger (see p. 53).

Chapter XXV

The evening before the wedding, Rochester is absent on business. Jane apprehensively waits for him in the orchard. She tells him that, the previous night, she dreamt of carrying an unknown child through the ruins of Thornfield. When she woke, a woman like the vampire was in her room. Jane lost consciousness, but next morning her veil was torn. Rochester reassures her that the woman was Grace Poole and tells her to sleep with Adèle.

Commentary: **Instead of telling the story chronologically, Brontë makes Jane withhold the knowledge of Bertha's visit until she tells Rochester, thus increasing tension and suspense.**

Context

Goethe's 'The Bride of Corinth', a Gothic horror story that features a female vampire, was published in translation in 1844 in *Blackwood's Magazine*, to which Reverend Brontë subscribed.

Chapter XXVI

The morning of the wedding, a grim-faced Rochester hurries Jane to the church. A stranger declares the existence of a previous marriage, and Mason, who has seen Jane's letter to her uncle, testifies that his sister still lives. Rochester takes them all to view his wife, imprisoned in the attic of Thornfield Hall and guarded by Grace Poole. Jane retreats to her room in despair and prays.

Commentary: **'Creole' is a term used for someone of European origin who was born in the West Indies, but can also refer to someone of mixed race. This ambiguity fostered nineteenth-century prejudices against different races. In the next chapter, Rochester tells Jane that he 'longed only for what suited me — for the antipodes of the Creole' (p. 358). The assumption is that Bertha is full of vices because she is a Creole. Bertha is bound to a chair, treatment that reminds the reader of Jane's own humiliation when she was locked in the red-room and the servants prepared to tie her to the chair; 'This preparation for bonds, and the additional ignominy it inferred, took a little of the excitement out of me' (p. 15). This echo of Jane's own vain struggles against oppression acts as a reminder of the similarities between the two characters.**

Chapter XXVII

Some hours later, Jane emerges from her room having decided that she must leave Thornfield. To persuade her that she would be morally right to stay, Rochester tells her about his arranged marriage and the consequences. She says farewell and asks God to look after him. That night she slips away and takes a coach as far as she can afford to go.

Commentary: **'You shall yourself pluck out your right eye; yourself cut off your right hand': there are many references to the Bible throughout this novel. This one comes from the Sermon on the Mount where Christ is condemning sexual misconduct. Jane judges that it is her heart that has offended and must be punished. This reference foreshadows Rochester's symbolic 'punishment' to his eye and his hand. Rochester assumes Jane will still live with him and, when she resists, he says 'Jane! Will you hear reason?... because, if you won't, I'll try violence.' He always expects women to give in to his demands and sees this as 'reasonable'. As Jane leaves Thornfield, Rochester has manipulated her into feeling guilty that she is 'the instrument of evil' to the man she 'wholly' loves.**

Chapter XXVIII

Two days later, the coach leaves Jane on the moors. She is comforted by nature, prays and sleeps well. Next morning, faint through lack of food, she walks to a nearby village, first asking for work and then begging for food. People are suspicious of a well-dressed beggar and shut her out. Eventually, she wanders to an isolated house on the moors and watches two young ladies through the window. Jane knocks; a servant refuses to admit her; she collapses and is rescued by St John Rivers.

Commentary: **Jane is set down at a crossroads, symbolic of choices she has to make. Praying for Rochester, Jane 'felt the might and strength of God' and 'convinced I grew that neither earth should perish, nor one of the souls it treasured'. This is a turning point for Jane as she becomes convinced by Helen's doctrine that God 'will never destroy what He created' (p. 97), and that even sinners like Rochester can be saved. Like Helen, Jane is tempted to embrace death to avoid 'further conflict', but this is not her creed and she struggles on, determined to take responsibility for herself.**

Chapter XXIX

Context

The closeness of the Rivers family reflects the closeness of Charlotte and her siblings.

For three days, Jane lies ill; when she recovers, she helps Hannah in the kitchen and learns more about her hosts. Old Mr Rivers, who has just died, lost his fortune through an unwise investment. His children have come home briefly to sort out his affairs, then Diana and Mary must return to their positions as governesses. St John is the local clergyman. Jane tells the family some of her story and admits that she has not told them her real name. St John agrees to find her work.

Commentary: **The man old Mr Rivers trusted was his brother-in-law, John Eyre.**

Chapter XXX

Jane lives very happily with Diana and Mary and she gratefully accepts St John's offer of a position as schoolmistress. The Rivers sisters and brother learn of the death of their wealthy but estranged uncle, but are disappointed in their hope that he planned to repair the wrong done to their father and leave them some of his fortune.

Commentary: **Like the Brontës' Aunt Branwell and Mr Brocklehurst, St John is a Calvinist, believing in predestination, that is, that some souls have already been elected for salvation and the rest are destined for damnation, or 'reprobation'.**

Chapter XXXI

On her first evening in her cottage, Jane struggles to overcome feelings that she is degraded by her occupation. St John comes and delivers a lecture about the necessity to 'turn the bent of nature' and explains why he wants to be a missionary. Rosamond Oliver arrives and it is obvious that he is struggling to repress his love for her.

Chapter XXXII

Jane settles comfortably into her new home but every night her passionate feelings for Rochester are released in dreams. On waking, she represses these longings and appears tranquil by the time school starts. Rosamond visits her, often when St John is teaching, and is impressed by Jane's sketches, asking Jane to sketch her portrait. Mr Oliver visits and invites Jane to Vale Hall. When St John sees the portrait, he tears a strip from the paper Jane uses as a hand-rest and departs mysteriously.

Two months after Jane left Thornfield, Bertha burned it down. At this time, Jane has settled into her new life as village schoolmistress, and she observes 'compared with that of a governess in a rich house, it was independent' (p. 408). Her feelings for Rochester are suppressed. However, Brontë reminds us of Bertha and the way she has been treated when Jane tells St John, 'solitude is at least as bad for you as it is for me'. The pictures Jane draws here suggest that she has found contentment in having, at last, a home and she has no need to imagine subjects.

Chapter XXXIII

St John returns next day in a snow storm, his suspicions that she is the missing heiress confirmed by her name on the paper. Delighted, she determines to share her fortune with her new-found cousins.

Commentary: **Brontë spins out the mystery by having St John tell the story slowly and teasingly rather than confronting Jane at once. This way the knowledge dawns on us slowly, so that we can empathise with Jane's pleasure at finding a family.**

Chapter XXXIV

Jane moves back to Moor House just before Christmas. She and Hannah spring-clean the house and Jane refurbishes it tastefully. St John disapproves of this waste of her talents. Jane teaches herself to read German, but St John asks her to help him learn Hindustani. She asks

Context

Jane is still legally a minor, so she needs two judges to approve her decision.

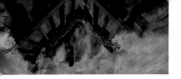

the solicitor vainly about Rochester and then writes twice to Mrs Fairfax, who does not reply. In May, St John asks her to accompany him to India as his wife. She is tempted by the idea of missionary work but agrees to go only as his companion. St John is deeply offended with her.

Commentary: **When Jane says 'since those days I have seen paysannes and Bäuerinnen', this is the only reference to Rochester's and Jane's travels in Europe.**

Jane's reaction to St John's proposal is worth noting. When he first asks what her heart says, Jane repeats her answer as if desperate to stop him speaking the dreaded words. However, Brontë describes her as 'struck and thrilled', suggesting that the prospect of sacrificing herself as a missionary excites her. When he asks her to come as his 'helpmeet and fellow-labourer', 'the glen and sky spun round; the hills heaved', as if she nearly faints. Her ambition tells her that being a missionary is 'the most glorious man can adopt or God assign', as if at last she has found the answer to her declaration that 'women feel just as men feel; they need exercise for their faculties, and a field for their efforts as much as their brothers do' (pp. 129–30). When St John tells Jane: 'Refuse to be my wife, and you limit yourself for ever to a track of selfish ease and barren obscurity', Brontë seems to be foreshadowing Jane's position at the end of the novel.

Chapter XXXV

St John rejects Jane's overtures of friendship and she repeats her refusal to marry him, claiming 'If I were to marry you, you would kill me. You are killing me now.' He is offended and shocked at her 'unfeminine' behaviour. A week later, she admits to being 'thrilled' by his evening prayers and almost yields to his will. She entreats heaven to guide her and, as if miraculously, hears Rochester's voice calling her name. She goes to her room and prays.

Commentary: **'God did not give me my life to throw away': in this her beliefs differ from Helen's. She has found her own interpretation of religion. The term 'castaway' shows that St John, like Brocklehurst in Chapter VII, fears she is already damned.**

Chapter XXXVI

Jane returns to Thornfield and finds it burned to a shell. The landlord of the Rochester Arms tells her that Bertha set fire to the house and then threw herself off the battlements, and that Rochester was maimed and blinded trying to rescue her.

Commentary: **Brontë keeps the reader in suspense as Jane walks to Thornfield and tells us her thoughts. Jane is a self-conscious narrator, deliberately shaping her narrative to prolong the suspense: 'Hear an illustration, reader'. Another method of drawing out the tension is to have the story eventually told in a long-winded and confusing way by old Mr Rochester's butler.**

Rochester's attempt to save Bertha is his first step towards his redemption. The fire is both a symbolic warning of the destructiveness of unrestrained passion, and also a means of purifying Rochester by punishing and redeeming him. It could also be argued that Jane's assertion of her independence requires the destruction of Thornfield as a symbol of male dominance.

Chapter XXXVII

Jane goes straight to Ferndean, teases Rochester out of his depression and encourages him to propose to her. She accepts, and he tells her of his prayer before crying out her name. The coincidence that he did this just as she heard his voice fills her with awe, but she does not tell him. He thanks God and entreats him to help him lead a purer life.

Commentary: **Unlike in Chapter XXIII, when Rochester manipulated Jane into declaring her love for him, this time Jane controls the conversation, makes Rochester jealous and forces him to declare his feelings first.**

Chapter XXXVIII (Conclusion)

Ten years later, Jane brings her supposed autobiography to a close, telling her readers that they married, are blissfully happy and have children. Adèle was sent to a more indulgent school and has become a pleasing young lady. Diana and Mary are happily married, and Jane and Rochester meet them once a year. Jane corresponds regularly with St John, who is dying but joyful at the thought of his reward in heaven.

Commentary: **For an analysis of this chapter see the 'Extended commentaries'.**

Context

While she was writing *Jane Eyre*, Brontë was caring for her father, who was having an operation to remove cataracts, so she knew what it was like to care for a blind man.

*Pause for **Thought***

Brontë gives Jane the statement 'Reader, I married him', rather than: 'We were married.' What does this suggest about how Jane thinks of their marriage?

Themes

Bildungsroman

a novel dealing with the early emotional, spiritual or educational development of its hero or heroine

...telling her story becomes her way of knowing herself and establishing her identity

As a **Bildungsroman**, the main theme of **Jane Eyre** is Jane's growth to maturity and her struggle to attain self-fulfilment. It is based on the Romantic concept of the self as individual and unique. She tells her story several times, to Mr Lloyd, Helen, Miss Temple, Rochester, St John and finally to the readers of her supposed autobiography. At first she struggles, because, as a child, she cannot analyse her feelings but, ultimately, telling her story becomes her way of knowing herself and establishing her identity.

Brontë inevitably draws on themes of education, religion, gender equality, social class, and the need to love and be loved. As Jane journeys through life, she experiences many crises that force her into crucial judgements and decisions, both conscious and subconscious. By the end, she has learned to balance nature and nurture, and she has found lasting happiness. Jane realises that, with St John as her husband, she would never be able to act naturally so, paradoxically, her freedom and independence are to be found in a relationship of mutual emotional dependence, where husband and wife come together as equals.

The dramatic tension that makes the novel so powerful is created because Jane is so frequently pulled in opposing directions. This means that it can be valuable to explore contrasting themes, although they are all interlinked and do not separate conveniently.

Rebellion versus conformity

In the first chapters, Jane rebels against unjust authority, demands liberty and her rights as an equal. She openly rebels against John Reed and his mother but finds that vengeance brings no lasting satisfaction. From Helen Burns, she learns the value of passive rebellion. Helen appears to submit to oppression and conform to society's expectations; however, when Miss Scatcherd beats her, she refuses to cry openly.

Pause for Thought

Why do you think Miss Scatcherd responds with 'Hardened girl!'? What was Miss Scatcherd trying to achieve?

At Lowood, Jane learns to mask her fiery, wilful, emotional nature under a coolly polite, submissive exterior. She has learned this lesson so well that she suffers greatly at Thornfield under Rochester's tyrannical efforts to force her to show her feelings for him. She hides them until he threatens her independence, declaring that she must stay, even after she discovers he is married. Even after she has agreed to marry him, she still appears to conform to society's expectations of a submissive wife, but actually manages to control him. Rochester observes: 'Jane, you please me, and you master me' (p. 301).

Some contemporary reviewers viewed the novel as politically subversive because, by claiming that every individual is important, Brontë was effectively advocating democracy.

Duty versus inclination

In order to maintain her integrity and be true to her essential self, which she calls her 'soul', Jane has to learn not to follow her inclination but to listen to the voice of duty. When she decides to leave Thornfield, she personifies this internal battle: 'Conscience turned tyrant, held Passion by the throat' (p. 343). Jane has another interesting struggle between duty and inclination when she writes about teaching at Morton School: 'I felt — yes, idiot that I am — I felt degraded'; however, she anticipates a time when she will be able to 'substitute gratification for disgust' (p. 414).

Reason versus feeling

The supporting characters often embody one or other of these opposites: St John consciously suppresses feeling, and Rochester considers what is reasonable to be what he feels is right. Just before Rochester proposes to Jane, we are invited to compare her with Eliza, who represents judgement without feeling, and with Georgiana, who represents feeling without judgement. Diana and Mary Rivers represent that harmonious balance between judgement and feeling that Jane needs to achieve.

After the fire in Rochester's bedroom, Jane admits to her feelings for him, but reason prevents her from imagining a fairy-tale happy ending: 'Sense would resist delirium: judgment would warn passion' (p. 177). After the broken wedding, Jane's reason triumphs over her love for Rochester. Later she is tempted to go with St John to India if she is convinced that it is God's will that she should marry him, but, in retrospect, Jane Rochester realises that 'To have yielded [to Rochester] would have been an error of principle; to have yielded now would have been an error of judgment' (p. 482).

In the end, Jane chooses passion, but only when Rochester has been through his ordeal by fire and he acknowledges 'the hand of God in my doom' (p. 514). Jane loves him more now that she can be 'really useful' to him, and so she has achieved that balance of passion and reason. She is no longer at risk of losing her individual identity in her overwhelming love.

> **Context**
>
> The literary critic Elizabeth Rigby wrote in *The Quarterly Review* in 1848:
>
> Altogether the autobiography of Jane Eyre is pre-eminently an anti-Christian composition. There is throughout it a murmuring against the comforts of the rich and against the privations of the poor, which, as far as each individual is concerned, is a murmuring against God's appointment — there is a proud and perpetual assertion of the rights of man, for which we find no authority either in God's word or in God's providence…

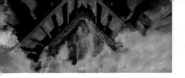

Earth versus heaven

Throughout the novel, Jane is presented with the dilemma of how to reconcile fulfilment in this life with a future in heaven. The early chapters of *Jane Eyre* give a clear impression of the intimidating way religion was taught in the nineteenth century. After Jane's passionate outburst, Miss Abbott tells Bessie: 'God will punish her: He might strike her dead in the midst of her tantrums', and to Jane she says: 'if you don't repent, something bad might be permitted to come down the chimney and fetch you away' (p. 16). Jane has been well indoctrinated; she tells Mr Brocklehurst that hell is 'a pit full of fire' into which the wicked fall and where they burn for ever (p. 39).

At Lowood, Helen has abandoned hope of earthly fulfilment and set her sights firmly on heaven. She tells Jane that her suffering on this earth will gain its reward in heaven, and so she teaches forgiveness of one's tormentors and acceptance of one's lot. Being a realist, Jane questions the very idea of heaven: 'Where is that region? Does it exist?' (p. 97). She cannot accept that life is merely a brief time of suffering before the better life to come. However, Jane is influenced by Helen's faith so that she is able to forgive Mrs Reed on her deathbed. At Thornfield, Jane falls into the trap of idolatry: 'I could not, in those days, see God for His creature: of whom I had made an idol' (p. 316). Rochester himself seeks salvation through Jane, but Brontë makes him find God before Jane can marry him.

The rigidities of institutionalised religion are satirised in the inflexible Mr Brocklehurst and criticised in St John Rivers, whose sermons are bitter and harsh. St John has rejected happiness in this life in favour of the next. He represses his natural instinct because he is convinced that he has to choose between religion and earthly love. St John's certainty that he will win 'his incorruptible crown' leads to his early death. A religion that excludes human affections is fit for heroes but Brontë demonstrates that it is not a creed to live by.

Jane is tempted by St John's choice of self-sacrifice but only because she has lost her hope of earthly happiness with Rochester. When Jane almost agrees to go with him to India as his wife, she acknowledges: 'I had now put love out of the question, and thought only of duty' (p. 482). She entreats heaven to show her the path, and that is when she has the strange psychic experience that calls her back to Rochester. However, before she returns to him, she prays. Jane's faith has developed into one based on individual conscience and the guiding influence of nature. She claims that Rochester's voice is 'the work of nature' (p. 483). For her, the proof

TASK 7

Find from the text how ten-year-old Jane plans to avoid being sent to hell.

Top ten *quotation* ❯

Context

Rochester is a good example of evangelical belief in individual regeneration. Finding faith after passing 'through the valley of the shadow of death', his Byronic cynicism gives way to religious acceptance and an acknowledgement of his responsibility for his troubles. On turning back to God, he is rewarded and finds happiness.

of God's existence is in her natural surroundings: 'it is in the unclouded night-sky, where His worlds wheel their silent course, that we read clearest His infinitude, His omnipotence, His omnipresence' (p. 373).

Nature versus society

It is a central tenet of the Romantic Movement that what is inherent and original in humankind is natural. Both humankind and nature are organic; they share a life force that allows them to develop and regenerate, as opposed to man-made worlds that cannot grow or reshape themselves. From the start of the novel, society is portrayed as at odds with nature. Society's artificial rules have marginalised Jane, because the family disowned her mother when she married beneath her. They forced Rochester, a younger son, into a marriage of convenience and prevented him from divorcing Bertha when she went mad. They pushed the impoverished St John into a career in the church rather than letting him fulfil his worldly ambitions.

Jane has a passionate nature, which she must learn to control. Helen Burns tells Jane that, although it may be natural to resist those who punish her unjustly, 'Christians and civilised nations disown it' (p. 69). Brocklehurst declares that 'we are not to conform to nature. I wish these girls to be the children of Grace' (p. 76).

Brontë follows the Romantic view but she does insist that following one's nature must be tempered by adherence to God's laws. When Rochester, following the Romantic view that one may justifiably rebel against social conformity, asks Jane to 'transgress a mere human law', Jane determines to 'keep the law given by God' (p. 365). When Jane falls in love with her employer, she must deny her nature. She warns herself to think of him only as her paymaster, but exclaims that this is 'Blasphemy against nature!' When Jane escapes from society onto the moors, she seeks refuge with 'the universal mother, Nature', and, when she hears Rochester's voice, she is convinced that 'it is the work of nature' (p. 483). God's laws are not at odds with nature, but society's are.

It may be natural for Jane and Rochester to marry, but Brontë does not try to reconcile the two opposing forces of nature and society. They live at Ferndean, secluded from society in a house that Rochester thought too unhealthy for Bertha because of its 'ineligible and insalubrious site' (p. 496). Jane has learned to reconcile her natural feelings with society's expectations, but Brontë is too much of a realist to imagine that society would change to accept her. There was no place in Victorian society for a marriage of equals.

> **Context**
>
> Victorian society regarded children as naturally bad and needing to be taught how to be good. By contrast, the Romantics, following Rousseau, regarded children as innocent and pure until corrupted by society.

❮ Top ten *quotation*

There was no place in Victorian society for a marriage of equals

Characters

Jane Eyre

Jane's name reflects her looks and her character. She is 'plain Jane', with no pretensions and no social status. Her surname has a number of **homophones**. She is her uncle's 'heir'. She is often compared with spirits of the 'air'. She is tempted to 'err' and learns from her experiences. 'Ire' is an approximate homophone that Brontë frequently uses; by Chapter XXXV Jane has learned not to attend to 'the suggestions of pride and ire', but they are still important factors in her personality.

Jane is an orphan whose father was a poor clergyman and whose mother was disowned by her parents when she married. The novel follows her development from a dependent child to a mature woman who has achieved self-knowledge, independence and marriage with her intellectual equal. We follow her life as her self-discipline and integrity are tested, as she learns to balance feeling and judgement, as she achieves independence and equality with the man she loves, and as she finds her own understanding of religion out of the different doctrines.

Jane is a total contrast to both Blanche and Bertha in her youth, petite stature, and intelligence, but Brontë seems to make her similar to Bertha in temperament. As a child, Jane is passionate and highly strung, and there are several references to her being 'mad' or unrestrained. Brontë shows her readers that Jane, like Bertha, is a passionate woman but that, unlike Bertha, she learns to repress her feelings. At Gateshead, Jane learns by experience that losing her temper does not make her feel better, but it is at Lowood that she learns to control her passionate feelings, and she is able to master 'the rising hysteria', when humiliated by Brocklehurst. Jane imbibed much of Miss Temple's habits so, when she goes to Thornfield, she appears quiet and self-disciplined.

Jane's personality is revealed to us through her memory, which enables her to see her life as a whole and make sense of it as she turns it into an 'autobiography'. It is by remembering and retelling her story that she learns to know herself, recognising her strengths and her weaknesses.

She is not well served by Brontë's narrative technique as she is used to voice the author's judgement on other characters. This means that she can appear cold and unfeeling when she writes about children, intellectually snobbish when she writes about Mrs Fairfax, Rosamond

---

homophones

words that sound the same but have different meanings and are spelt differently

---

TASK 8

Find quotations in which Brontë has Jane admit that she was savage and ungovernable.

---

*Pause for **Thought*** ⏸

If you have watched one of the film versions, consider how faithfully both Jane and Mr Rochester have been presented.

Oliver and the children at her school, too quickly judgemental when she describes Mason and, to a modern reader, full of racial prejudices when she writes about Adèle's 'French defects', the 'ignorant' Indians and the 'enslaved' in Eastern cultures.

Edward Rochester

Brontë was an avid reader of Lord Byron's poetry and became fascinated by his male heroes. In almost every respect, Rochester is a Byronic hero. He is dark and brooding rather than good-looking, and he is of muscular appearance, rather than tall and elegant like a conventional romantic hero. On his first appearance, he certainly looks the part. He is mounted on a 'tall steed' and accompanied by a 'great dog', both suggesting male virility. However, Brontë immediately breaks the mould and makes him fall from his horse. He loses his dignity and independence and is forced to rely on Jane for help. This signals that Brontë's treatment of her Byronic hero may not be entirely admiring.

Rochester is arrogant, domineering and brusque; a fiery and lawless outsider, he is isolated, bitter and cynical, although he can put on an act of jovial conviviality. Mystery surrounds him, and he is corrupted by secret guilt, yet he burns with remorse. Through Jane, Brontë shows disapproval of his behaviour, but lets him preserve the traces of a noble spirit and the ability to inspire love. Rochester does not treat women with respect. Bertha he married for money, lived with as man and wife until he inherited the estate, and then disposed of her in what he thinks is a humane fashion. Then he travelled but tells Jane that he hates the time he spent in Europe: 'Hiring a mistress is the next worse thing to buying a slave: both are often by nature, and always by position, inferior: and to live familiarly with inferiors is degrading' (p. 359).

However, like Byron's heroes, he accepts responsibility for his actions. He takes responsibility for Adèle when her mother abandons her, even though she is not his daughter, and he brings his wife to Thornfield rather than incarcerating her in an asylum. Like Byron's heroes he has travelled restlessly to escape the past, but Brontë invites us to condemn his affairs when Jane rebukes him. In his conversations with Jane, he asserts his right to get pleasure out of life and declares: 'I know what my aim is, what my motives are; and at this moment I pass a law, unalterable as that of the Medes and Persians, that both are right' (p. 161).

Brontë explores the ideas of individualism and self-determination represented by Byron's heroes but through her heroine she condemns them. Instead of perpetuating the philosophy of the Byronic hero,

Context

The seventeenth-century Earl of Rochester was a brave soldier, a brilliant satirist and a libertine who despised society's attitude to sex. Brontë was probably thinking of him when she chose the name for her hero. Rochester is also the name of a city, so the character is linked by his name with the landed gentry.

*Pause for **Thought***

Is the fact that he says he hates the time he spent in Europe evidence that he is now ashamed of the way he treated these women?

Context

Daniel 6:15 reads: 'Then the men went as a group to the king and said to him, "Remember, O king, that according to the law of the Medes and Persians no decree or edict that the king issues can be changed."'

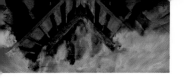

Brontë rewards her hero only after he gives up his determination to create his own future. By the end he has learned to take responsibility for his own actions and to live within the confines of God's laws.

Context

Brontë's father studied at St John's College, Cambridge, which had strong evangelical connections.

St John Rivers

St John, like his namesake, becomes a disciple, devoting his life to God's work. His surname suggests the river in which the early disciples were baptised, which strengthens the contrast between St John and Rochester.

We are told that St John is like 'the warrior Greatheart, who guards his pilgrim convoy from the onslaughts of Apollyon' (p. 521). In *The Pilgrim's Progress,* Bunyan tells us that Apollyon was 'a foul fiend'. Like Rochester, St John battles against 'foul fiends', but his are different. As a man, he faces the demons of worldly ambition; as a missionary, his fiends are ignorance, war, bondage, superstition and fear.

A year before he meets Jane, St John was 'intensely miserable' because he thought he had made a mistake in his choice of career. Like Rochester, St John is also associated with fire but, whereas Rochester burns with sexual desire, St John burns with a desire for glory and power. However, once his father lost everything, he redirected his passion into the service of God. He claims to have suppressed sexual desire, but he admits to Jane that he loves Rosamond wildly. He dismisses his feelings as 'a mere fever of the flesh', claiming to be 'a cold, hard man' (p. 432), because he thinks he has effectively repressed his natural feelings. On the surface he appears cold and so is often associated with images of snow and ice, or of stone.

His hope is that being a missionary will satisfy his ambition; he labours not for love of his fellow man but for the 'incorruptible crown' that awaits him in heaven. He has determined to subjugate everything to this one ambition, refusing to relinquish his plans for love, for his sisters or for his duties in the parish. His repetition of the first person possessive determiner signals his egotism when he says: 'Relinquish! What! my vocation? My great work? My foundation laid on earth for a mansion in heaven? My hopes of being numbered in the band who have merged all ambitions in the glorious one of bettering their race' (p. 431).

*Pause for **Thought***

If you have watched one of the film versions, discuss how faithfully St John has been presented.

He observes Jane closely, testing her character, with a view to marrying her to assist him in his ministry. He is hurt by the scorn she pours on his proposal the first time he asks her; the second time he is visibly pained, and yet he perseveres and gently tries a third time to persuade her. Perhaps Jane is misjudging him; perhaps he feels for her more than he admits.

Whereas Rochester appeals to Jane's need to love and be loved, St John appeals to that side of her nature that aspires to something great and which wants to sacrifice itself to the service of God. The fact that Jane ends her autobiography with a eulogy of St John shows how important ambition is to her, but this occupation is only 'the one best calculated to fill the void left by uptorn affections and demolished hopes' (p. 466). Whereas St John offers duty, sacrifice and a place in heaven, Rochester offers love and a home, both of which the orphan has craved throughout the book. She is only superficially similar to St John, whereas of Rochester she says that she is 'bone of his bone, and flesh of his flesh' (p. 519).

Other characters

Diana and Mary Rivers

Diana, Roman goddess of chastity, and Mary, mother of Jesus, are names that suggest purity. Jane's cousins are women whom Jane admires and with whom she feels in perfect sympathy.

The Reed family

Brontë makes structural parallels between the Rivers and Reed families. Both are related to Jane; the father is dead, there is one son and two daughters. Both family names begin with 'R' and are associated with water. However, whereas reeds are weak and bend easily in the current, rivers flow strongly, bringing life to the land and its people.

Because the Reeds are shown filtered through Jane's resentment, they are totally unsympathetic characters, and do not emerge as rounded characters. However, Jane does begin to pity Mrs Reed as she lies dying. Mrs Reed was jealous of her husband's love for his sister, Jane's mother, and so she resents having to look after her orphaned niece. Mrs Reed also feels guilty because she did not bring Jane up as if she were her own child, as her husband had made her promise on his deathbed. Jane's outburst spelled this out to her and, when Mrs Reed lies to her brother-in-law, John Eyre, it is done out of revenge for Jane's childish attack. Her breaking of her deathbed promise to her husband and her lie to his brother torment her final hours, so she is unable to accept Jane's offer of reconciliation.

Jane's cousins take their lead from their mother, and they not only exclude her, but John actually bullies her. Choosing the same name for the sons emphasises the contrast: whereas John Reed is weak and amoral, St John is strong and fiercely moral.

> *Pause for **Thought***
>
> In appearance Rochester and St John are a total contrast, but can you find any similarities between them?

…the Reeds are shown filtered through Jane's resentment…

…whereas John Reed is weak and amoral, St John is strong and fiercely moral

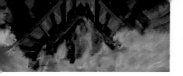

Miss Temple

Miss Temple is Jane's first role model and, like a temple, she provides a sanctuary for the orphan child. Miss Temple is an elegant, beautiful, cultured woman, compassionate and fair-minded. She listens to Jane's version of the events at Gateshead, verifies it, and clears her name before the whole school. It is from Miss Temple that Jane gains her passion for self-improvement. She also learns self-control from Miss Temple, who has an equally passionate sense of injustice and hatred of hypocrisy. She knows, however, when resistance could be worse than useless and her face turns to marble as Brocklehurst rebukes her for her kindness to the girls. While Miss Temple is at Lowood, Jane regards it as home, but, once she is married, it becomes imprisoning and she desires liberty.

Helen Burns

Context

Helen was based on Charlotte's oldest sister, Maria, who contracted tuberculosis at school and died. Charlotte described Maria as having a 'prematurely developed and remarkable intellect, as well as…mildness, wisdom and fortitude'.

Helen Burns's name links her with the fire imagery of the novel. She burns with religious fervour, and she also burns with indignation; her dirty fingernails and untidy drawers suggest she is a rebel at heart. However, instead of struggling against injustice, she looks forward to death as a release from this life. On her tombstone is inscribed the word 'Resurgam', declaring that she will rise again, like a flame from the ashes.

Like St John, Helen has sublimated her passion into religious ecstasy but, whereas St John is ambitious for glory, Helen's religion is one of self-denial. She epitomises Christ's teaching of loving your neighbours and turning the other cheek, as she endures Miss Scatcherd's bullying without complaint, even admitting culpability. However, this can be read as a form of passive resistance that actually goads her persecutor to be more cruel and puts herself in the role of martyr.

didactic with the intention of teaching the reader and instilling moral values

When Jane first meets her, Helen is reading Samuel Johnson's *Rasselas*, a **didactic** romance in which Samuel Johnson, the writer and lexicographer, philosophises about the vanity of this world. He argues that surrender and self-control will enable us to bear with the difficulties of life. Helen is dying of tuberculosis and embraces the idea of death as a release from the harshness and injustice of life on earth. She offers a contrasting form of belief to the harsh creed of Brocklehurst, being convinced that salvation is open to all. She is an inspirational character with a lifelong influence on Jane.

Mr Brocklehurst

plosive a stop consonant released quickly (p, b, t, d, k, g)

The **plosive** consonants in 'Brocklehurst' sound prickly and hard. Brock is a common name for a badger, which is fierce and tenacious.

Brocklehurst is presented through the eyes of a ten-year-old child, and so he appears a caricature of a pompous, self-righteous hypocrite. We are invited to see him as a black pillar, cold, hard and unbending, with features like those of the cruel wolf in *Little Red Riding-hood*. We are invited to laugh at his insistence that the girls should be shorn of curls and wear plain, unflattering clothes, while his own family are overdressed and wear artificial curls. However, there is something sinister about the way he inspects the girls' underwear on the washing line and tries to suppress their emerging womanhood with inadequate food and insubstantial childish uniforms.

Brocklehurst's behaviour reveals that this supposedly charitable institution is there not for the benefit of the girls, but to perpetuate the injustice in society and fit them for the humble roles assigned to them. He acts as a contrast both to Helen, whose faith totally contradicts his, and to St John, who preaches the same doctrine, but who lives by what he preaches.

Bertha Mason

Bertha is never developed as a character. We learn her history through Rochester's biased narrative, and we see her only after she has been 'embruted' by ten years of solitary confinement in a windowless room with no mental stimulation. Her presence is not essential to the plot, only the fact that Rochester is married, so her role in the novel is largely symbolic. She has been variously interpreted as representative of the British Empire's attitude to other cultures, as symbolic of the Victorian wife, trapped in the home, or as a manifestation of Jane's subconscious feelings of rage against injustice and fear of her sexual desires, which she has learned to suppress. Bertha acts as a warning of the consequences of a woman allowing passion to rule her behaviour.

Bertha's most important function is to be the Gothic horror element and to raise the suspense through her preternatural laugh, her blood-sucking vampiric behaviour and her goblin appearance. When Bertha is finally revealed, she is introduced by Rochester as 'bad, mad and embruted' (p. 337), and described by Jane as an 'animal' and a 'hyena' (p. 338). Although Bertha appears to be just like a caged animal, Brontë hints at the unhappy woman who is not allowed a voice. In the first mention of Bertha's 'tragic' laugh, Jane uses the adjective 'preternatural' to suggest something Gothic and beyond the range of nature, but she also recognises the tragedy of the person laughing.

Bertha escapes from her gaoler three times. The first time she sets Mr Rochester's bed alight; and the next time we hear of Bertha, she has attacked her brother, who was complicit in arranging this traumatic

Context

Charles Dickens threatened to have his wife committed to an asylum when she raised objections to his affair with a young actress.

TASK **9**

Write Bertha's account of the time she escaped and visited Jane's bedroom. Try to echo specific aspects of Brontë's form, structure and language as far as possible. You should also write a brief commentary explaining how you have tried to reflect the original novel.

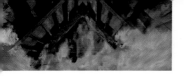

Pause for Thought ⏸

How far does Brontë intend us to believe that Bertha has been turned into a brute by her mental illness and how far by the brutalising treatment she has suffered? Is it madness or despair to set fire to your gaoler's room (what had happened the evening before?), then to seek out your rival's room and set fire to that, then to climb to the roof and throw yourself to your death?

Pause for Thought ⏸

Why do you think Brontë has made Blanche similar to Bertha?

Taking it
Further

Read an imaginative account of Grace Poole's story on www.bbc.co.uk/drama/janeeyre/grace_poole_1.shtml

marriage and does nothing to protect her from her husband. Her words reveal thought behind her action: 'She said she'd drain my heart.' The second time Bertha escapes, she rips Jane's wedding veil, but she does not try to harm Jane. Two months after Jane left, Bertha escaped from her prison for the last time. She set fire to Grace Poole's room next to her own; and then to the bed in the room that had been Jane's. She then climbed to the roof and, as Rochester approached, 'she yelled, and gave a spring, and the next minute she lay smashed on the pavement'.

Blanche Ingram

Blanche is French for white, with connotations of coldness and lack of feeling. Rochester compares Blanche to Bertha before he married her, suggesting that Bertha also was beautiful, arrogant, cruel to her social inferiors and self-willed. He feels no qualms about falsely arousing Blanche's expectations to make Jane jealous, saying, 'Her feelings are concentrated in one — pride; and that needs humbling' (p. 303), revealing his misogyny in declaring that women should be humble.

We are told that Blanche's 'mind was poor' (p. 215) and Bertha's cast of mind was 'common, low, narrow' (p. 353). Both women set out to seduce Rochester. Jane observes that Blanche coins her smiles lavishly, flashes her glances unremittingly, and manufactures elaborate airs; Rochester describes how Bertha 'flattered me, and lavishly displayed for my pleasure her charms and accomplishments' (p. 352).

Mrs Fairfax

When her clergyman husband died, Mrs Fairfax accepted a position as housekeeper to a distant relative. She is kind and warm-hearted and she acts as a substitute mother to Jane, warning her to be on her guard when Rochester proposes. Brontë uses her as a plot device to provide limited information about Thornfield, its owner, and his guests.

Grace Poole

Grace is the woman hired from the Grimsby Retreat by Rochester to guard and take care of his first wife. Grimsby Retreat is based on the Quaker York Retreat in which the mentally ill were cared for with humanity. Grace does not mix with the other servants and she takes her responsibility seriously, although occasionally Bertha escapes. Jane is told that Grace is responsible for the strange noises and sinister happenings, but Grace watches out for her, warning her to bolt her door.

Rosamond Oliver

The name Rosamond comes from the Latin 'Rosa Mundi', meaning 'Rose of the World', and is appropriate to someone who is not only beautiful, but also a good person. 'Oliver' suggests an olive branch, which is a biblical symbol of peace and, in classical mythology, sacred to Venus, goddess of love. Jane is intellectually snobbish towards Rosamond, declaring her 'not profoundly interesting or thoroughly impressive' (p. 425), so readers must judge for themselves whether in this Jane is a reliable narrator. Rosamond is not merely charming, she is a true philanthropist. She has persuaded her father to finance schools for the children of the poor and she has furnished the schoolmistress's cottage and paid for the education of a servant.

Unlike the other rich characters in the novel, Rosamond is not snobbish. She flirts with St John but is sensitive and thoughtful, rebuking herself when she remembers that he will be sad because his sisters have had to leave. It seems that she does not really love St John, however, because, when he makes clear his intention to go to India, she marries the grandson and heir to Sir Frederick Granby. Since her grandfather was a journeyman needlemaker, Brontë is using her to represent the rapid rise of the families of working class entrepreneurs in the Industrial Revolution.

> …Brontë is using Rosamond Oliver to represent the rapid rise of the families of working class entrepreneurs in the Industrial Revolution

Servants

Brontë has a keen ear for the dialogue of servants, which helps her to depict them economically but realistically. They have an important function in keeping the sometimes extraordinary events of the novel rooted in the ordinary world. Mary and John, at Ferndean, talk in a broad Yorkshire dialect; they are stolid and loyal, pragmatic and 'phlegmatic'. Hannah also speaks broad Yorkshire, but she loves to talk and is fiercely protective of the Rivers family.

Brontë uses no dialect features for the servants at Gateshead, presumably to differentiate servants in big houses from those lower in the hierarchy. Miss Abbott, the lady's maid, reflects her mistress's prejudices and preferences, but Bessie does try to stand up for Jane. She is the one person Jane clings to when she leaves Gateshead. Bessie is a warm, good-hearted girl, although quick to scold and, before she leaves, Jane learns to appreciate her essential kindness and not to be afraid of her.

Bessie's ballads and folk-lore stay with Jane throughout the novel and are a significant influence on her imagination. Bessie visits Jane at Lowood and tells her about her uncle's visit, thus preparing us for the time when her aunt summons her. When she revisits Gateshead, Bessie's warm welcome provides a sharp contrast to the coldness of the Reed family.

> **Context**
>
> Sir Walter Scott wrote historical novels set in Scotland and made it acceptable to use local dialects in novels.

Form, structure and language

Form

Brontë originally structured *Jane Eyre* in three volumes. Volume One ends after the fire in Rochester's bedroom, when Jane is left deliriously happy, trying to resist the temptation that the promised land is in sight. Volume Two opens with her tremulous hopes of seeing Rochester, only to learn that he has left the house. Volume Two ends with Jane in despair after learning of Rochester's marriage and seeing his wife.

*Pause for **Thought***

Why do you think Brontë chose to break off at these two places in the story?

Since *Jane Eyre* is supposedly a fictional autobiography, the reader is invited to identify and sympathise with Jane and view events from her point of view. We share Jane's thoughts and feelings as she grows up and are invited to understand her anxieties and her longings. However, while we appear to be experiencing the story through the mind of a young person, it is actually a mature woman who is recreating it for us. Brontë creates the illusion that Jane relives her life, remembering how she thought and felt when events took place.

> Brontë selects only those incidents that she considers relevant to her theme

Jane Rochester is supposedly able to select and shape the incidents of her life, guiding our attitudes and passing judgements on her own imperfect understanding as a child. However, Jane declares that 'this is not to be a regular autobiography: I am only bound to invoke memory where I know her responses will possess some degree of interest' (p. 99). Brontë selects only those incidents that she considers relevant to her theme. We are given Jane's own subjective account of her development. However, we also learn about the subconscious parts of her personality through her paintings and her dreams, visions and presentiments.

A first-person narrative, written with hindsight, could be flat and dull if the writer does not employ techniques to create the appearance of spontaneity and to preserve the mystery. Brontë wants her readers to experience events as Jane had, with her limited knowledge and understanding. To this end she withholds the information that her narrator is actually Jane Rochester until the final chapter, and the mature

Jane tells her story with only occasional observations on events. Jane is aware of her readers, sometimes addressing them directly, but she gives no hint of the final outcome. At some key points, she employs the present tense to give events a dramatic immediacy, but Brontë usually uses the past tense to suggest that Jane is remembering what happened.

Nevertheless, we are made aware that the mature Jane still feels the pains of her childhood, telling her readers 'I never forgot the, to me, frightful episode of the red-room…nothing could soften in my recollection the spasm of agony which clutched my heart…' (pp. 84–5). Although Jane is aware of her subjective judgements, she has still not left them behind. When she moves into Morton School and feels 'degraded' by the step, it is in the present and future tenses that she tells her readers: 'let me not hate and despise myself too much for these feelings; I know them to be wrong — that is a great step gained; I shall strive to overcome them' (p. 414). She does not, however, appear to be aware of the way her love for Rochester affects her judgement. When we finally meet Bertha, and Rochester grapples with his wife before tying her up and binding her to a chair, Jane admiringly says 'He could have settled her with a well-planted blow; but he would not strike: he would only wrestle' (p. 339).

Play-like features

At the beginning of Chapter XI, Brontë compares a new chapter in a novel with a new scene in a play, and some scenes read very like a play. When Jane meets Rochester dressed as a gypsy, for instance, every little detail of the conversation is recorded, even when Rochester pauses to find the best way of putting into words what he believes to be Jane's feelings for him, and she interrupts with 'I what?' In a first-person narrative, it is difficult for a novelist to reveal the thoughts of other characters, so Brontë employs various strategies such as when she makes Rochester speak his thoughts aloud, regardless of the fact that Jane is listening. His speech when he drops his gypsy disguise reads more like a soliloquy, especially when he admits his weakness in the face of his desire for Jane: 'So far I have governed myself thoroughly. I have acted as I inwardly swore I would act; but further might try me beyond my strength' (p. 233).

Limitations of a first-person narrative

One of the problems with a first-person narrative is that it is difficult for the writer to guide the reader's opinions. The narrative is supposedly filtered through Jane's memory, but Jane loves Rochester and wants to believe in him. Brontë, however, has allowed the facts to speak

TASK 10

Choose another scene that reads like a play. How has Brontë achieved this dramatic quality?

Rochester's speech when he drops his gypsy disguise reads more like a soliloquy…

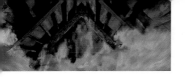

for themselves. In Chapter XXVII, Rochester tells Jane the details of his previous marriage and subsequent behaviour. Since he is our sole informant for much of his narrative, we have to accept it, but we can recognise the positive spin he puts on his story, trying to portray himself in an admirable light. He freely admits that he married Bertha for her money, although he blames his father and brother, and, while he needed her money, he lived with her as man and wife. However, when his father died four years later, he was rich enough not to need her any more. He could not divorce her, so he locked her up. He tells Jane that Bertha's 'vices sprang up fast and rank: they were so strong, only cruelty could check them; and I would not use cruelty' (p. 353), and yet he imprisons her in a room without a window, which is empty except for a fire and a lamp.

Structure

Brontë's choice of a quasi-autobiography for the form of her novel gives it an essential unity in spite of the different settings. The structure of the novel is organised around Jane's quest for her own identity, with each of its five parts representing a different stage in her development. This means that Brontë omits the first ten years of Jane's life and starts Jane's autobiography with the incident that marks the first time she has resisted John's bullying and fought back. We are introduced to Jane as she is about to leave Gateshead and embark on her growth to maturity and her struggle to attain self-fulfilment.

At the beginning of Chapter X, Brontë briefly summarises eight years of Jane's life and the narrative skips to the point where she begins to feel restless at Lowood and takes her future into her own hands. We are then given an apparently continuous narrative of the next two years. In the final chapter, the 'Conclusion', the narrative skips another ten years and the book comes full circle and ends at the point where Jane tells us that she has finished writing her autobiography and claims to be 'supremely blest', having achieved the self-fulfilment she sought. However, although St John's death is imminent, he is still alive, and Jane devotes the final page of the book to her ambivalent feelings about him, suggesting that she has aspirations and ambitions that have yet to be fulfilled.

Place names

As in the allegorical *The Pilgrim's Progress,* Brontë has used significant place names. They are all compound words with appropriate associations and/or metaphorical meanings. Jane's journey begins at 'Gates-head', an image suggesting that it is her mind that is confined. Metaphorically, the gate is shut, but Mr Lloyd opens it, and she can start on her journey.

Her journey to Lowood seems to be 'of preternatural length' (p. 50), reflecting her anxieties. Lowood Institution is literally low, built in a 'cradle of fog and fog-bred pestilence' (p. 91), and metaphorically it is a place where the orphan daughters of impoverished gentlemen are prepared for their humiliating position in society. Just before Jane leaves, Bessie tells her 'You are genteel enough; you look like a lady' (p. 108), so, with Miss Temple as her role model, obviously the school has failed to humble her, although she has learned self-control.

She approaches Thornfield apprehensively, and this is where she is most strongly tested. Rochester is being appropriately punished at Thornfield for his sins, and Jane's self-control is tested in a number of ways on this field of thorns. The Gothic mansion with its battlements, its mysterious third storey and the apparently inexplicable noises and events all symbolically dramatise the uncertainties and anxieties of her subconscious.

After her hopes are dashed, Jane travels to an unknown destination where she experiences a profound religious experience on the moor. She considers suicide, rejects it and, having escaped from the Slough of Despond, crosses the marsh and finds a family at Marsh End. The name of the house is Moor House, where she experiences true freedom, symbolised by the moor. However, once again she is in a repressive patriarchal regime and has to escape. This recurring pattern ends symbolically with the destruction of Thornfield.

By contrast, Ferndean is buried deep in a wood. As she approaches, it is like a labyrinth, 'so thick and dark grew the timber of the gloomy wood'. The trees were 'close-ranked' and 'all was interwoven stem, columnar trunk, dense summer foliage — no opening anywhere' (pp. 496–7). This symbolises the doubts and difficulties surrounding her quest. Brontë adapts the *Sleeping Beauty* story as she fights through to rescue the dormant Rochester. However, the gloomy setting holds no terrors for her and, once she has penetrated the barrier, 'Fern' has positive associations with growth, gentle nature and the fresh, relaxing colour green. A 'dene' is a narrow wooded valley, so the name not only describes the location but also implies that the place is natural, not shaped by humans; as Jane says 'no flowers, no garden-beds' (p. 497). Jane and her husband are secluded from society and can live according to their true natures.

Context

When God expelled Adam and Eve from the Garden of Eden, he condemned them to a life of thorns and thistles.

*Pause for **Thought***

Why do you think Brontë intends her readers to draw a comparison with the fairy tale of the Sleeping Beauty as Jane approaches Ferndean?

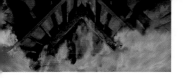

TASK 11

Find other examples where Brontë prepares the reader for events to come.

Foreshadowing

The unity of this novel is greatly enhanced by the frequent use of foreshadowing to prepare us for something that will happen later. Perhaps the most important example is the hints we are given of Jane's eventual inheritance, which brings her financial independence and a family. In Chapter III, Jane tells the apothecary of some 'poor, low relations called Eyre', then, in Chapter X, Bessie visits Jane and mentions that her father's brother appeared at Gateshead seven years before, looking for her. In Chapter XXI, Jane learns that her uncle had written to her aunt three years earlier, reporting that he had been successful in Madeira and expressing his desire to adopt Jane and make her his heir. Mrs Reed wrote to Mr Eyre telling him that Jane had died of typhus fever at Lowood. These hints prepare the reader for St John's revelation.

TASK 12

Draw a table to give a timeline for the novel, showing how Brontë uses the weather and the seasons to further the action or enhance the mood of the scene.

Weather

Another structural device that aids the unity of the novel is Brontë's use of the weather and the seasons to further the action or enhance the mood of the scene.

Language

A network of connecting images, symbols and themes supports the narrative and enhances the cohesion.

Imagery

TASK 13

Find other examples of the weather being used metaphorically.

As well as using weather literally, Brontë also uses it figuratively in similes and metaphors. For instance, in the image: 'A Christmas frost had come at midsummer; a white December storm had whirled over June' (p. 341), Jane reveals that, just as a winter storm will destroy all the signs of summer, so the news of Rochester's previous marriage had, in a sudden blast, destroyed all Jane's hopes of happiness.

Pillars and columns

Several times Brontë compares Brocklehurst with a statue, a pillar or a column, reinforcing the impression that he is cold and unfeeling. St John is also compared with a statue and a column, and Jane seeks to penetrate his 'marble breast' (p. 428); however, like Jane, he burns with an inner fire.

Miss Temple is also linked with a marble column when Jane observes that, as Brocklehurst spoke, 'her face, naturally pale as marble, appeared to be assuming also the coldness and fixity of that material; especially her mouth, closed as if it would have required a sculptor's chisel to open it' (p. 75). Clearly Miss Temple is another angry woman who is outraged at Brocklehurst's words but, unlike Jane, she will never voice her anger. She has repressed her passions and become a sanctuary, a 'temple'.

> …Miss Temple is another angry woman who is outraged at Brocklehurst's words

Birds

In contrast to these images of hard, cold stone, Jane and Rochester are both compared with birds. Jane observes Rochester's 'full falcon-eye flashing' (p. 314) and, at Ferndean, he reminds her of a 'caged eagle, whose gold-ringed eyes cruelty has extinguished' (p. 498). A few pages later, she uses the same image, comparing him with 'a royal eagle, chained to a perch…forced to entreat a sparrow to become its purveyor' (p. 507). His injuries and his angry frustration make him seem like an eagle chafing at his captivity. He is now dependent on her, a common sparrow, small, plain and ordinary; this analogy reveals the importance she places on appearance and her awareness of her own plainness. To Jane, Rochester seems like a noble bird, powerful, dominant and fierce, but the reader will extend this comparison, noting that falcons and eagles are predators that have no pity for their victims.

Taking it Further ➤

Compare the engravings of the peregrine falcon and the linnet from Bewick's *History of British Birds*, which you will find in the downloads of resources for this literature guide on www.philipallan.co.uk/ literatureguidesonline

Jane is always linked with small, insignificant-looking birds. As Rochester describes his feelings when he first saw her, he compares her with a nimble, fragile-looking, but courageous linnet. At Ferndean, he cannot see her and compares her with a skylark, a bird that delivers a beautiful song so high in the sky that people can barely see it. By association, the reader gleans that Jane may seem fragile, but she is determined and her voice brings joy to the blinded Rochester.

At particular times, Brontë extends this imagery and Rochester compares Jane to a caged bird. Soon after he arrives, he says, 'I see at intervals the glance of a curious sort of bird through the close-set bars of a cage: a vivid, restless, resolute captive is there; were it but free, it would soar cloud-high' (p. 162). Just before he proposes, he urges her 'Jane, be still; don't struggle so, like a wild, frantic bird that is rending its own plumage in its desperation.' Her reply rejects the comparison and asserts her equality as a human being: 'I am no bird; and no net ensnares me; I am a free human being with an independent will, which I now exert to leave you' (p. 293).

After the broken wedding, when he is desperate for Jane to stay, the imagery suggests that he is contemplating taking her by force:

> **Consider that eye: consider the resolute, wild, free thing looking out of it, defying me, with more than courage — with a stern triumph. Whatever I do with its cage, I cannot get at it — the savage, beautiful creature! If I tear, if I rend the slight prison, my outrage will only let the captive loose. (p. 366)**

Although to a twenty-first century reader rending the prison could refer to violating her body, Brontë meant that Rochester recognises Jane's free spirit, enclosed within a cage of convention. Not only is she a woman, she is also a governess and so unable to speak her mind or fulfil her ambitions. The jealousy he has aroused in her reveals the depth of her feelings to him, but she is still unable to voice them and can only declare her independence. By the time she learns of his previous marriage, the cage has become her protection and it is her belief in her principles that prevents him from persuading her to stay.

To Jane, birds are symbolic: she uses them to explain her feelings at having to abandon Rochester. When she hears birdsong on the moors, she observes 'birds were faithful to their mates; birds were emblems of love' (p. 369). She tells us that her heart, 'impotent as a bird with both wings broken...still quivered its shattered pinions in vain attempts to seek him' (p. 373). So to Jane a bird is a symbol of love in its constancy and her love in particular because, just as a bird with broken wings cannot fly to its mate, Jane's 'principles' will not allow her heart to seek out the man she loves.

Symbolism

In literature, a symbol combines an image with a concept. We have seen, for instance, how Jane took the image of a bird and used it to explain the concept of love. Whenever we read a literary text, we bring our previous experience with us, so a writer knows that images will evoke particular associations in our minds. When Brontë uses imagery, she expects us already to have ideas about what these images represent. When the same or similar images are used frequently throughout the novel, they achieve a particular resonance and increase in power.

Fire and ice/heat and cold

These opposing images are ones that Brontë frequently evokes. At Gateshead, when Jane is looking at Bewick's *History of British Birds*, she

---

Not only is she a woman, she is also a governess and so unable to speak her mind or fulfil her ambitions

Top ten *quotation* ❭

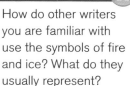

remembers particularly the bleak, cold vignettes that tell stories of death and disaster rather than the pretty or amusing ones. The cold, desolate images reflect her isolation at Gateshead and the lack of warmth in the family. At Gateshead, Jane's burning indignation and desire for love were met with cold repression, rejection, isolation. After the confrontation, Mrs Reed's 'eye of ice continued to dwell freezingly' on Jane (p. 44), whereas by contrast Jane observes that, 'A ridge of lighted heath, alive, glancing, devouring, would have been a meet emblem of my mind' (p. 45). When she first arrives at Lowood, Jane tells her readers, 'The fury of which she [Helen] was incapable had been burning in my soul all day' (p. 88). However, here she learned to suppress her inner fire, and she achieved a temperate harmony.

Both the red-room and the drawing room at Thornfield Hall are described as chilly through disuse. Both rooms have looped curtains, mirrors, ottomans and a pale marble mantelpiece; both rooms are furnished in crimson and white. Jane writes of a 'general blending of snow and fire' (p. 123), as she describes the drawing room at Thornfield, suggesting that here, too, she will feel strong passions and also desolation.

After Rochester confides in her about Adèle's past, Jane cannot sleep. She muses on the fact that he no longer takes 'fits of chilling hauteur', and that, for her, 'his presence in a room was more cheering than the brightest fire'. While she lies thinking, she hears a 'vague murmur, peculiar and lugubrious', and, as her door was touched, 'I was chilled with fear' (pp. 171–3). After she has doused the fire, 'Strange energy was in his voice; strange fire in his look'. By this time, however, Jane is 'cold' (p. 177). Gradually, fire has come to represent 'passion', while cold has come to represent 'sense' and 'judgment'. Both of these are elements of Jane's personality, and the main theme of the novel is how she learns to reconcile the two apparent opposites. Rochester is 'Vulcan' (p. 509); after Jane refuses to stay with him, 'He seemed to devour me with his flaming glance: physically, I felt, at the moment, powerless as stubble exposed to the draught and glow of a furnace' (p. 365). By contrast, St John seems to be carefully controlled ice, declaring that he is 'a cold, hard man' (p. 432).

Jane tells Rochester that St John is 'cold as an iceberg' (p. 511). However, St John tells Jane that, a year before, he 'burnt for the more active life of the world' (p. 416) and, when he saw Rosamond Oliver, Jane saw 'his solemn eye melt with sudden fire, and flicker with resistless emotion' (p. 420). By using this contrasting imagery, Brontë is showing her readers that, although Jane and St John appear to be opposites, they both burn with inner desires.

*Pause for **Thought***

How do other writers you are familiar with use the symbols of fire and ice? What do they usually represent?

*Pause for **Thought***

Is it coincidence that, just as Jane is admitting to her growing passionate love for Rochester, fire threatens to consume him?

Context

Vulcan was the ancient Roman god of beneficial fire and also destructive, devouring fire, including the fire of volcanoes. He became patron of blacksmiths.

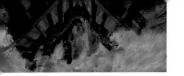

At times, Brontë juxtaposes the two extremes of fire and ice. For instance, when St John claims that, 'I am cold: no fervour infects me' (p. 443), Jane responds with 'I am hot, and fire dissolves ice.' St John has tried to suppress his passions and become icily impervious to passion or persuasion. Jane recognises that his coldness is only assumed and that, if she is persistent, he will give her an answer. However, Brontë uses these recurring images to reinforce the contrast between them and how wrong it would be for Jane to marry St John. Jane recognises that as his wife she would be 'forced to keep the fire of my nature continually low, to compel it to burn inwardly and never utter a cry, though the imprisoned flame consumed vital after vital' (p. 470).

The chestnut-tree

Jane tells us of the great tree and how it is struck by lightning on the evening when Rochester defies God and society to propose to her. This ill omen gives the readers an uneasy feeling that their love is to be similarly blasted, although we do not know of Rochester's secret.

Brontë gives the chestnut-tree a symbolic status that becomes more significant for the reader as events unfold. As she waits for Rochester anxiously after Bertha had torn her veil, Jane notices that, although it is split in two, the 'cloven' halves were still joined together at the roots. The word 'cloven' is the past participle of 'to cleave', which has opposite meanings of to split apart and to cling together. She speaks to the two halves of the tree as if they are two people in a relationship, 'the time of pleasure and love is over with you: but you are not desolate: each of you has a comrade to sympathise with him in his decay' (p. 319). It seems like a premonition that Jane and Rochester are going to be violently split asunder, but they will remain joined at 'the faithful, honest roots'. The importance of this symbol is that it suggests that the bond between the two lovers is natural. Together with the lightning strike, it suggests that there is something elemental about their passion.

In the penultimate chapter, Brontë once again uses the tree as a symbol. Rochester sadly says 'I am no better than the old lightning-struck chestnut-tree in Thornfield orchard' (p. 512), but Jane is back with him; like the tree, their relationship has a 'firm base and strong roots'. Jane responds with 'You are no ruin, sir — no lightning-struck tree: you are green and vigorous'. Her optimism is well-founded as, in the final chapter, we learn that, ten years later, he has children who, like the plants around the tree, 'grow about your roots...and lean towards you, and wind round you'.

...the symbol of the chestnut-tree...suggests that the bond between the two lovers is natural

Moon

The moon is also introduced casually at first, although at key points of the novel, and gradually it achieves a symbolic status. It might be more appropriate to refer to the moon as a character rather than a symbol, as Jane always refers to it with the feminine pronouns 'she' and 'her'. The moon gives Jane light to dress by as she leaves Gateshead and helps to comfort her after her humiliation by Mr Brocklehurst. Its light guides her to Miss Temple's room when Helen is ill. The moon 'was waxing bright' when Jane first met Rochester, and she is 'not at all afraid of being out late when it is moonlight' (p. 134). This supportive presence seems to take an active role when Mason is attacked as, even before he screams, Jane tells us she 'looked in at me' and 'her glorious gaze roused me'.

The moon is present when the tree is struck by lightning, and it appears in the fissure created by the two halves of the tree as Jane speaks to them. This time the moon is disturbingly ominous but Brontë has withheld the reason: 'her disc was blood-red and half overcast; she seemed to throw on me one bewildered, dreary glance, and buried herself again instantly' (p. 319). Eventually we learn that Jane is waiting for Rochester to return so she can tell him about the night-time visitor who tore her wedding veil. Brontë has projected Jane's puzzlement and anxiety on the moon, to create anticipation in the reader. Even before Bertha appeared, Jane had a prophetic dream that Thornfield was a ruin (p. 325), and she wandered there 'on a moonlight night' carrying a little unknown child that clung to her, almost strangling her, until she fell from the crumbling wall.

After she breaks from Rochester, Jane has a dream of being in the red-room at Gateshead. The strange light that had frightened her as a child, precisely because it was not the moon, seemed to mount the wall and pause in the centre of the ceiling; 'the gleam was such as the moon imparts to vapours she is about to sever'. This time the light seems to become the moon, and Jane watches with anticipation, 'as though some word of doom were to be written on her disc'. However, in her dream, when the moon broke through the clouds, it had metamorphosed into a white human form that gazed on her and whispered in her heart, 'My daughter, flee temptation!' She answers 'Mother, I will' (p. 367). Here the moon has become a projection of Jane's own need for reassurance about her own worth.

Jane sees the moon as a support, someone who advises her wisely. In this passage, it seems that the moon has become the mother she never had. Perhaps, however, the moon is, for Jane, the eye of 'the universal mother, Nature' (p. 372). As she settles to sleep on the moors after

Context

The moon has long been a source of curiosity and wonder for humans, seeming to be full of mystery and magic. It appears at night, the time of sleep and dreaming which seems close to death and the afterlife. It is also often associated with love and romance.

*Pause for **Thought***

What do you think the child might symbolise?

...the moon has become a projection of Jane's own need for reassurance about her own worth

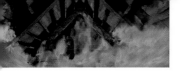

fleeing from Thornfield, Jane rises to her knees to pray: 'Night was come, and her planets were risen' (p. 373). Her fears are calmed, and she feels safe. She has a strong awareness of God, saying 'it is in the unclouded night-sky, where His worlds wheel their silent course, that we read clearest His infinitude'. Brontë seems to suggest that perhaps the moon is more than a recurring motif because Jane sees it as the visible symbol of God's presence.

This attribution of human qualities to nature is often called the pathetic fallacy, the arousal of feeling by misleading means. Ruskin criticised this kind of personification as 'morbid', but Brontë here shows how valuable a device it can be for revealing aspects of a character's personality, especially in a first-person narrative, and for heightening the dramatic tension.

Context

John Ruskin coined the phrase 'pathetic fallacy' to comment on 'the difference between the ordinary, proper, and true appearance of things to us; and the extraordinary, or false appearances, when we are under the influence of emotion, or contemplative fancy'.

Bertha

As well as being a vital character in the novel, Bertha has a symbolic function. Jane hears the strange laugh while she is feeling frustrated at the way women are treated in a patriarchal society, suggesting that Bertha represents Jane's alter ego, her passionate self. When Bertha escapes and sets fire to Rochester's bed, Rochester has been confiding in Jane, telling her about Céline Varens. Bertha's fire could be intended to be symbolic of Jane's own sexual desire, which Brontë could not overtly express. This tête-à-tête in the garden has kindled her love for him and perhaps the dousing of the fire in Rochester's bedroom is a symbolic dousing of the fire of her dangerous passion.

The next time we hear of Bertha, she has attacked her brother. This attack comes just after Jane and Rochester have become more intimate after his impersonation of a gypsy. Jane has admitted to him 'I'd give my life to serve you' (p. 236). Once again her desire is breaking through the self-restraint. Bertha seems to be a symbol of what happens to a woman if she allows her desire to control her.

The second time Bertha escapes, she rips Jane's wedding veil. Rochester seems to fear Bertha's jealousy as he tells Jane to share Adèle's bed. As Adèle slept, Jane 'watched the slumber of childhood — so tranquil, so passionless, so innocent… [s]he seemed the emblem of my past life; and he I was now to array myself to meet, the dread, but adored, type of my unknown future day' (pp. 329–30). So, just as Adèle represents her passionless past, perhaps Bertha represents her fears of her own sexual passion. When Jane looks in the mirror, she sees Bertha throw the veil over her own head. It seems that, by using the device of the mirror,

Brontë is reinforcing the idea that Bertha is Jane's passionate, sexual, but necessarily hidden, self.

When Bertha is finally revealed, she is bound to a chair — treatment that reminds the reader of Jane's own humiliation when she was locked in the red-room. Because she struggled, Bessie and Miss Abbot prepared to tie her to the chair, and 'This preparation for bonds, and the additional ignominy it inferred, took a little of the excitement out of me' (p. 15). This echo of Jane's own vain struggles against oppression acts as a reminder of the similarities between the two characters.

Two months after Jane leaves, Bertha escapes from her prison for the last time and sets Thornfield alight. At this time, Jane has settled into her new life as village schoolmistress, and she observes 'compared with that of a governess in a rich house, it was independent' (p. 408). Her passionate feelings for Rochester are being firmly suppressed. However, Brontë reminds us of Bertha and how she was treated when Jane tells St John (p. 428) 'solitude is at least as bad for you as it is for me.'

The red-room

The red-room is a recurring motif that appears as a memory whenever Jane makes a connection between her current situation and that time of humiliation, exclusion and imprisonment. When Jane tells Miss Temple what happened at Gateshead, she explains to her readers that she never forgot 'the spasm of agony which clutched my heart when Mrs Reed spurned my wild supplication for pardon, and locked me a second time in the dark and haunted chamber' (pp. 84–5). She remembers Mrs Reed's rejection as a physical pain, and there is a strong suggestion that the adult still feels that pain.

Another time, after deciding that she must leave Rochester, Jane supposedly writes: 'I dreamt I lay in the red-room at Gateshead; that the night was dark, and my mind impressed with strange fears' (p. 367), only this time the strange light is the moon. The red-room becomes symbolic of what Jane must overcome in her struggle to find freedom, self-respect and a sense of belonging. She must overcome the male assumption of superiority embodied first in John Reed, then Brocklehurst, and then Rochester. She must come to terms with her own passions and sexuality, find a balance between reason and feeling.

> It seems that... Brontë is reinforcing the idea that Bertha is Jane's passionate, sexual, but necessarily hidden, self

> The red-room becomes symbolic of what Jane must overcome in her struggle to find freedom, self-respect and a sense of belonging

Contexts

Biographical context

Context

Patrick, the son of an illiterate Irish tenant farmer, changed his name from Prunty or Brunty to Brontë, which means 'thunder' in Greek. Brilliant and determined, he gained a scholarship to Cambridge University. Mrs Gaskell maligned him in her biography of Charlotte, having listened to malicious gossip from the nurse who lost her job when Elizabeth came to stay. Those who knew him agree that he was a devoted husband and father and a kind and affable man.

Context

William Wilberforce (1759–1833) was a British politician and philanthropist. He led the movement to abolish the slave trade.

Brontë drew upon her own experiences for *Jane Eyre*, and its power comes from the fact that she poured her own passionate feelings into her heroine. However, it is not autobiographical. Petite, plain, well-read and clever, Charlotte, like Jane, was a strong woman with an overwhelming capacity for love, a deep religious faith, and a well-developed sense of duty. Unlike Jane, however, she grew up in a very close-knit family.

Charlotte, born in 1816, was the third of six children of the Reverend Patrick Brontë and his wife, Maria. She was five when the family moved to Haworth, but soon afterwards her mother died of cancer. The children were then cared for by their aunt, Elizabeth Branwell, who had come from Cornwall to nurse her sister.

School

The older girls were sent to a new school, Cowan Bridge, specifically designed for the daughters of clergymen and supported by many eminent people, including Patrick's former university friend and sponsor, William Wilberforce. Although Charlotte's account of Jane's time at Lowood Institution is clearly based on her own experiences, it is enhanced by scandalous reports of other schools she had read in newspapers, and the picture is a caricature, written through the eyes of a child who clearly resented the school.

©Pictorial Press Ltd/Alamy

Charlotte Brontë

Nevertheless, the girls were unfortunate to be at the school during its difficult early years and, as at Lowood, there was an outbreak of typhus that masked the fact that Charlotte's older sisters were suffering from tuberculosis. As soon as Patrick knew of their illnesses, he took them all home but Maria and Elizabeth did not recover. This was a sadness that affected Charlotte deeply, and it also gave her a new sense of duty and responsibility as the oldest in the family.

Angria and Gondal

After this tragedy, the children were educated at home, enjoying the freedom of playing on the moors and happy in each other's company. They had a happy, normal, stable childhood, with an affectionate aunt and a father willing to spend time with them and join in their games. They made up plays, acting them out exuberantly and writing down their adventures. These plays developed into a complex imaginary world with two kingdoms, Angria and Gondal. They made tiny books out of scraps of paper and they imitated print in tiny writing that adults would not be able to read without a magnifying glass. They practised drawing by copying pictures such as the engravings in Bewick's *History of British Birds*.

They read avidly, and their father allowed them free run of his library. He did not censor their reading material at all, so they read works that, at the time, were considered too immoral for ladies, such as Byron's *Don Juan*. They also read books from libraries and periodicals such as *Blackwood's Magazine*, a miscellany of satire and comment on contemporary politics and literature, which was a strong formative influence, providing characters and settings for many of their games.

Patrick was a respected poet and writer and consequently a significant role model. He was also a tireless campaigner for social reform, so the children were not isolated from the world and its problems, nor from the appalling poverty that surrounded them. The curacy of Haworth was intended to be a step up in a glittering career; the fact that Reverend Brontë stayed is testament to his commitment to his parishioners and his determination to improve their lives.

The children were aware of what was happening in the world at large and incorporated real people and events into their stories. These imaginary worlds were not a retreat from reality but a source of endless fun, which they still enjoyed when they were adults. The books were strongly derivative, imitating those writers they enjoyed, such as Lord Byron and Sir Walter Scott. Charlotte used her characters to poke fun at her brother and sisters, developing the satirical skills she was to use in *Jane Eyre*.

> **Context**
>
> *Blackwood's Magazine* offered its readers a controversial but popular mixture of satire, reviews, criticism (both barbed and insightful), essays, fiction (including horror) and poetry.

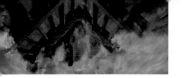

Patrick Brontë gave his children a thirst for education and the freedom, as far as he could afford, to find it wherever they could. Although their formal education was partial and fragmented, the Brontës came from a household where all kinds of artistic pursuits were encouraged. They tried their hands at everything, shared everything and explored human feelings in a way that would not have been possible without siblings who were kindred spirits.

Responsibility

In 1830, Patrick fell seriously ill, and the family realised that, if he were to die, the children would have no home and no income. At 14, Charlotte was again sent away to school to equip her to earn her own living. She was sent to Roe Head, and she soon settled in and made lifelong friends. She took seriously her responsibility to improve herself and was soon top of her class. Being extremely short-sighted, she could not play ball-games nor read the music to play an instrument, but she soon found her niche, telling horror stories in the dormitory and organising plays. Her two best friends, Ellen and Mary, often invited her to their homes and they remained close for the rest of her life.

Ellen Nussey and Mary Taylor appealed to the contrasting aspects of Charlotte's personality, which are central to *Jane Eyre*. Ellen unquestioningly accepted the current social and moral codes, reconciling herself to a life of duty and dependence; Charlotte strove to emulate her in her peaceful acceptance of her fate as a poor clergyman's daughter, unlikely ever to marry. In contrast, Mary Taylor was intellectually curious and totally careless of the opinions of others. Mary's letters and her example stimulated Charlotte to use her abilities and talents to the full and to question the prejudices of society.

At 16, Charlotte left Roe Head and returned to Haworth, slipping back easily into their imaginary kingdoms of Gondal and Angria. In 1835, however, she accepted a position as teacher at Roe Head, where she stayed until 1838. Disliking teaching, she made her first attempt to embark on a literary career, sending some of her poems to the Poet Laureate, Robert Southey. His reply reflected the prejudices of the time: 'Literature cannot be the business of a woman's life and it ought not to be. The more she is engaged in her proper duties, the less leisure will she have for it, even as an accomplishment and a recreation.' At the time, Charlotte took Southey's advice to heart, shelved her literary ambitions temporarily, and went back to teaching.

Nevertheless, she continued to write the imaginary stories of Angria, in which the women fall abjectly in love with her imaginary hero, the Duke of Zamorna, who treats them with an amused and cynical contempt. Rochester certainly owes something to his fictional predecessor but, unlike her Gondal stories, Charlotte rebukes him through Jane for his treatment of his mistresses and Blanche, and demands his pity for Bertha. *Jane Eyre* blends this romantic world of Charlotte's imagination with her sense of duty and her strong religious faith.

She took a series of positions as governess, where she gained more material for her novel. Charlotte hated the fact that she was treated as a servant; she found it exhausting and depressing to be constantly in demand, and she was doubtless a reluctant and melancholy governess. Still believing that she could not make her living by writing, the only escape seemed to be for the sisters to set up their own school at Haworth.

Pensionnat Heger

Accordingly, in 1842, Charlotte and Emily went to a school in Brussels to improve their language skills, and Charlotte returned later as a teacher. It was here that she learnt the rigours of the academic discipline needed for writing, and here that she experienced the passion that she dreamed of for her heroines, falling in love with the husband of Madame Heger, the director of the school.

On first seeing M Constantin Heger, Charlotte wrote:

> **He is professor of rhetoric, a man of power as to mind, but very choleric and irritable in temperament; a little black being, with a face that varies in expression. Sometimes he borrows the lineaments of an insane tom-cat, sometimes those of a delirious hyena; occasionally, but very seldom, he…assumes an air nor above 100 degrees removed from mild and gentlemanlike…**

In 1845, the three sisters submitted to a publisher a combined anthology of poetry. They wrote under the ambiguous pseudonyms of Currer, Ellis and Acton Bell, partly to preserve anonymity, but also to avoid the inevitable condescension and shock, because they 'had a vague impression that authoresses are liable to be looked on with prejudice'. When these failed to sell, each sister started to write a novel. Charlotte's first novel, *The Professor*, based heavily on her Angria stories and her experiences in Brussels, was rejected by a succession of publishers, but one of them encouraged her to continue writing.

Context

When Charlotte was proposed to by Ellen's brother because he needed a wife to take care of his pupils, she rejected him, because she would have lost her independence, and, like Jane, she needed to marry for love.

Context

Charlotte worked as a governess for the Sidgwick family at Stonegappe Hall, near Skipton, in 1839. She tried governessing again with the White family of Upperwood House, Rawdon.

Context

M Heger was the first person to observe Charlotte and Emily and realise their exceptional talents. His remarkable system of education and his stimulation worked as a catalyst for the sisters' inspiration for writing.

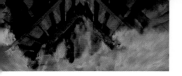

Literary success

For her next novel, *Jane Eyre,* published in 1847, Charlotte used local stories of mad wives locked away, and she based the descriptions of the buildings where Jane lived on houses she had visited. She drew on her own experiences and released all the pent-up feelings of her love for M Heger, her anger and grief at Cowan Bridge School for her sisters' deaths and her bitter resentment and sense of injustice at the way she had been treated as a governess. These strong emotions gave the novel a new and compelling power, which made it an instant success.

Almost a year after *Jane Eyre* was published, Charlotte's brother, Branwell, died of tuberculosis, complicated by alcoholism. A few weeks later, Emily died, followed a few months after that by Anne; both of them also dying of tuberculosis. Caring alone for her elderly father, Charlotte continued to write, publishing *Shirley* in 1849 and *Villette* in 1853. Eventually she found the love she craved and married Arthur Bell Nicholls, her father's curate, in 1854. She rejected him at first, as she had three earlier suitors, but his love was strong and he finally won her round, in spite of her father's objections. Charlotte became pregnant, but she was 38 and suffered violent nausea. She was nursed devotedly by her husband but grew progressively weaker and died just three weeks before her birthday.

Historical context

The nineteenth century was a time of great change:

- There were intense debates about religious issues, not least the question of who should hold authority in matters of religion.
- It was also a time of social reorganisation and the transfer of power as a new wealthy middle class, created by the Industrial Revolution, emerged to challenge the dominance of the traditional landowners.
- It was a time of heated controversy over ideas of democracy and political rights, fuelled by such significant events in the world as American Independence, with its Declaration of Human Rights, and the French Revolution, with its ideas of Liberty, Equality and Fraternity.
- It was a time of growing unrest among the working classes, who demanded relief from the appalling conditions in which they had to live and work and, gradually, the beginning of concern among higher classes for the plight of the poor.

The government, fearing that revolution would break out in Britain as well as abroad, brought in repressive legislation rather than trying to improve matters. Several times they suspended habeas corpus, the right not to be imprisoned without trial.

They were determined to protect and defend the landed interest, which was the basis of the government's political power. Common land on which people used to have the right to graze their animals was enclosed. Corn Laws were introduced to keep the price of grain high for landowners and to prevent the import of cheap grain from abroad; this kept the price of bread high. Game Laws were passed, which meant that anyone catching a rabbit, for example, to feed his starving family, could be transported for seven years. The authorities brought in the military to suppress civil rights demonstrations.

Nevertheless, pressure for reform grew and the first Reform Act was passed in 1832. This effected some minor improvements, but ordinary working men were still without a vote. The demand for universal male suffrage and a secret ballot acted as a rallying standard for working class agitation throughout the country. Marches, rallies, speeches and petitions were organised in support of it. Eventually, in 1884, the Third Reform Act was passed, giving the vote to male householders and lodgers who had been resident for twelve months. This still left a third of all men (including soldiers in barracks, policemen and domestic servants) without the vote.

Taking it Further ➤

In 1817, George Cruikshank drew a cartoon depicting the politician Lord Castlereagh suspending liberty from a printing press in reaction to the suspension of habeas corpus. See it on www. historyhome.co.uk/c-eight/distress/liberty.htm

Context

In 1819, at least 11 people were killed and 500 wounded when the yeomanry used sabres to break up a peaceful meeting on St Peter's Fields near Manchester. This outrage is popularly known as the Peterloo Massacre.

Social context

The Industrial Revolution

In the early eighteenth century, the British textile industry was largely based on wool, spun and woven by outworkers in their own homes. Spinning wheels and handlooms can produce only a limited amount, and the quality is not consistent, so new technology was invented to improve efficiency. As large, powered machines were developed that increased production dramatically, it was more efficient to house them in mills, and so, towards the end of the century, the whole industry was revolutionised. The increased demand for wool led landowners to evict their tenants so they could rear sheep. The outworkers found themselves unemployed and many weavers, calling themselves Luddites, took out their resentment on the machines. Many people moved to the towns in search of work.

Context

The Luddites named themselves after Ned Ludd, the Leicestershire man who had led the first rioters in the destruction of machinery.

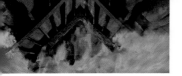

The Chartists drew up a list of six demands, including universal male suffrage and a secret ballot. They presented three major petitions to parliament in 1839, 1842 and 1848; all were refused outright.

However, there was famine in Ireland, and so desperately hungry people were flocking into England, also looking for work and prepared to take very low wages. This meant that whole families had to work to earn enough to keep them alive. The poor mill workers had no hope of changing the system through the political process, since only landowners had the right to vote, so a movement arose to bring about change by more direct means. These people drew up a six-point charter and so became known as the Chartists. Gradually the industry became regulated. In 1833 and 1844, for instance, the first laws concerning child labour were passed. For example, children were not allowed to work at night, nor for longer than twelve hours a day.

Haworth

The Brontë's home, Haworth, was a comparatively small town in the middle of the West Riding woollen industry, but it was important because it lay on one of the main routes between Yorkshire and Lancashire. Haworth is situated in the hills above Keighley and Bradford, with an ample supply of water, so it was an ideal place to site factories. When the Brontës moved to Haworth in 1820, it already had 13 small textile mills, as well as a large number of hand-loom weavers working in their own homes and a substantial cottage industry of wool combing. With the aftermath of the Napoleonic Wars and the industrial movement from the rural districts to the town, the population was rising sharply, bringing unemployment, misery and revolt.

HAWORTH'S MAIN STREET.

Overcrowding, poor housing, lack of sanitation, no running water, low wages, poor standards of nutrition, ignorance and lack of effective medical treatment all contributed to the spread of disease. With no running water in Haworth, people had to fetch water from one of the few pumps, and in summer the pumps ran so slowly that people had to start queuing in the middle of the night to get water for the morning.

The workers and their families lived in small houses in cramped streets. There was no sanitation at all, no sewers and few covered drains. The liquid waste, including that from privies, ran along open channels and gutters down the streets, and solid waste, also including the refuse from privies, was thrown into walled enclosures in the backyards, known as middensteads. These were emptied by farmers and used to manure their fields, but sometimes the middensteads would overflow, creating an even worse health hazard.

Life and death

It is estimated that tuberculosis accounted for a quarter of all deaths. Other major killers were typhus, cholera and influenza, which were more or less endemic, but frequently reached epidemic proportions. Other diseases such as measles, whooping cough and diphtheria were also endemic. In Haworth, 'wool-sorter's disease', which we now know as anthrax, was also virulent. As well as disease, the bad living conditions and ignorance led to food poisoning, and bad diet led to rickets, which could cause contracted pelvises, making childbirth difficult and even dangerous. Death in childbirth was also common due to puerperal fever, spread by the unwashed hands of the doctor or midwife.

With no unemployment benefit, no sick-pay and no pensions, people needed children to support them through illness and old age, so families were large and children sent out to work from the age of five or six. This led to another common cause of death or crippling injury in children. Children earned only 10% of an adult wage, and so mill-owners liked to employ children as cheap labour. They were forced to work very long hours, without breaks, and tiredness and hunger frequently led to accidents with the machinery. The smallest children were employed as 'scavengers' to creep under the machines, while they were still in operation, to gather up bits of loose cotton or wool. Whenever the wool trade was struggling, conditions grew even worse for the poor.

On 14 August 1842, about 10,000 people gathered at a Chartists' rally on Lees Moor, within sight and sound of Haworth. The military were called out to disperse the meeting, arresting and even shooting some

Context

There were no water closets in Haworth and only 69 privies, one of which was at the rectory. Most households shared a privy with up to 23 other families. No wonder the mortality rates were among the highest in the country.

Context

Life expectancy was low; 30% of children died before they reached their first birthday, 40% before reaching their sixth birthday, and the average age at death was only 25.

Context

In May 1830, when Charlotte was 14, about two-thirds of the workers of Haworth were unemployed and the rest were on short weeks.

Taking it Further

Learn more about the Babbage Report from http://freepages. genealogy. rootsweb.ancestry.com/ ~jeffreywright/ Babbage%20Report

of the demonstrators. A couple of weeks later, desperate mill workers sabotaged machinery by removing the plugs that powered the looms; this led to the formation of the Anti-Plug Dragoon Regiment. In *Jane Eyre,* Brontë mentions the demonstrations when Rosamond Oliver tells St John that she has been dancing with the officers of the –th regiment, brought in to suppress the riots.

Reverend Brontë worked tirelessly to relieve the suffering of the poor, and he repeatedly petitioned the General Board of Health to improve sanitation. His strenuous efforts to raise public subscription for the relief of the poor always failed because it was felt that relief should be given from public rates and not private charity. The poor were regarded as an underclass whose degradation was their own fault. It was frequently asserted that God had made them poor, and that he wished them to remain poor.

Eventually, when the overcrowded graveyard was contaminating the already unhealthy water supply, the Board commissioned the Babbage Report in 1850 and, as a result of this, conditions began to improve.

Brontë's feelings

On p. 129 of *Jane Eyre*, Brontë uses an electrical image to reveal her awareness of the potentially explosive nature of the rebellions fermenting in society: 'Nobody knows how many rebellions besides political rebellions ferment in the masses of life which people earth.' After demonstrations in 1848, she wrote in a letter that the government should 'examine carefully into their causes of complaint and make such concessions as justice and humanity dictate'. Nevertheless, she was not a revolutionary. In the same year she wrote to her former headmistress: 'convulsive revolutions put back the world in all that is good, check civilisation, bring the dregs of society to the surface…That England may be spared the spasms, cramps, and frenzy-fits now contorting the Continent and threatening Ireland, I earnestly pray!'

Class consciousness

Nevertheless, the social effects of the Industrial Revolution were not all doom and gloom. For the energetic and enterprising few, it offered opportunities for wealth that lifted former working class men up to a new middle class. From here they could socialise with and marry into the old-established landed gentry and aristocracy. Brontë illustrates this through Mr Oliver, whose father had been a journeyman needlemaker, but who was now able to boast that his daughter, Rosamond, married the grandson and heir to an aristocrat.

The tension created by these two sets of values is central to *Jane Eyre*. On the one hand there are rationality, rebellion and individualism; on the other hand are tradition, conservatism and piety. Class consciousness pervades every part of the story. Jane's mother was from landed gentry but she married beneath her, a poor clergyman, so Jane struggles against her poverty to maintain the status she believes is her right.

Brontë's own position was even more precarious than that of her heroine, as her father came from Irish peasantry. Perhaps this is why she portrays Jane as reluctant to fall back, in social terms, concerned that, by becoming the teacher at Morton, she had 'taken a step which sank instead of raising [her] in the scale of social existence' (p. 414). It seems that, rationally, Charlotte believed in equality but all her life she had been striving to lift herself out of the social position into which she had been born, and she had not managed to reconcile the conflict between the deeply embedded traditional social mores and the radical views she had acquired.

Governesses

As wealth shifted from the traditional landowners to the owners of industrial and mercantile enterprise, the latter not only began to challenge the privileges and superior social status of the upper class but also to consolidate their position against the threat from the working classes. They used institutions such as the church and the school to keep those whom they regarded as social inferiors in their place. The new industrial middle classes also exploited the offspring of the impoverished gentry, by employing them as tutors or governesses, in order to lift their own children up above the class their parents had been born into.

It is Rochester who voices Brontë's opinion of 'this governessing slavery' (p. 311). On the one hand, Brontë was a realist, recognising the need to earn her own living and wanting independence by whatever means she could gain it. On the other hand, she was well read and had a creative imagination, which gave her a feeling of superiority over those with less intellect than herself. She reveals how difficult she found it to reconcile the two, as her heroine finds herself torn between reason and feeling, between realism and imagination.

Taking it Further ▶

Read Anne Brontë's novel *Agnes Grey* to learn more about the miseries of life as a governess.

The position of women

There was much debate on the Woman Question. Nevertheless, even though there was a queen on the throne, this made no difference

to the legal and economic position of other women. They had little more power or standing than children. No woman could vote and the law ignored them. Legally, a woman belonged to her nearest male relative. When a woman married, any property she owned became her husband's, and, if she earned any money, that was her husband's also. If she did not marry, after her father's death she became a dependant of her nearest male relative.

Whereas, thanks to industrialisation and the growth of the servant class, more working-class women than ever before worked outside the home, conditions were poor and wages too low for them to achieve any independence. Middle-class women were allowed no economically productive careers. They were not permitted to go to university, to enter the learned professions or to engage in business. A middle-class woman was expected to stay at home until she married and then spend the rest of her life looking after her family. If, like Charlotte and her heroine, she did not come from a wealthy family and circumstances meant that she had to earn her own living, she was permitted to teach, but teachers and governesses were poorly paid and looked down upon by society.

Education

There was usually no opportunity for working-class girls to gain any education at all, but Brontë shows in Rosamond Oliver's school that this situation was beginning to change. Middle-class girls were taught various social accomplishments to impress prospective suitors and to occupy their time, but their minds were not stretched and they were not expected to take these pursuits seriously.

Brontë's rejection of the status quo can be seen, not only in her own published works, but also in the fact that Jane paints to express her imagination and individuality rather than to create a portfolio to impress an employer. However, when Jane chooses a school for Adèle, she conforms by selecting one that made her 'a pleasing and obliging companion — docile, good-tempered, and well-principled' (p. 519).

Expectations of women's behaviour

At Thornfield, Jane makes a strongly worded demand for equality with men, which reveals the social expectations of women's behaviour in the middle of the nineteenth century (pp. 129–30). A woman was supposed to be passive, quiet and obedient, entirely subject to the authority of her male protector. She was not supposed to be ambitious or to aspire to anything more than being a wife and mother. English women were not expected to show any strong emotion such as anger or love, and it was most definitely assumed that they did not feel any sexual desire.

Women were idealised as the custodians of family values. While men could go out and 'enjoy' themselves, women stayed at home, upholding morality and truth, remaining uncontaminated by male desire, providing a calm and virtuous refuge for the men to return to. In *Jane Eyre*, Brontë challenges these contemporary assumptions by offering a heroine who is at least as intelligent and passionate as Rochester, and who surpasses him in intellectual and artistic aspirations.

> **Context**
>
> Foreign women were considered to be more highly sexed. It is no coincidence that Rochester's mistresses were all foreign.

Cultural context

Religion

The nineteenth-century Church followed the Old Testament, teaching that 'Every motive, thought, word and deed will be under close scrutiny in the Day of Judgement'. Although God was deemed to be merciful, in the interest of universal justice he was still expected to punish every unrepentant sinner on the Day of Judgement. For the obedient believer, it was promised that this day will usher in eternal glory, but the unbeliever was warned that it will be a day of anguish and annihilation.

For people living in the first half of the nineteenth century, death was an integral part of life; they never knew where it would strike, nor how quickly, so it was important to them to prepare for the life after this one. The Church exploited this fear in an attempt to make people submissive and uncomplaining. For the majority, life in this world was hard and unrewarding, but the Church promised them their reward after death: 'Blessed are the meek: for they shall inherit the earth' (Matthew 5:5).

'Self-righteousness is not religion'

Established religion was used as a form of social control to keep the poor in their place and prevent them from rebelling against the establishment. At Lowood, the girls are taught humility and self-sacrifice, supposedly for the good of their souls. Mr Brocklehurst's children, however, are not taught the same lessons, so clearly the real reason was to prevent the orphaned children of poor gentlemen contravening social mores by trying to climb out of their humble positions. The

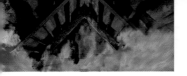

established church was firmly committed to supporting the government in preserving the existing class divisions.

When the novel was criticised for being 'an insult to piety', Brontë replied in her preface:

> **Conventionality is not morality. Self-righteousness is not religion. To attack the first is not to assail the last. To pluck the mask from the face of the Pharisee, is not to lift an impious hand to the Crown of Thorns.**

> **...narrow human doctrines, that only tend to elate and magnify a few, should not be substituted for the world-redeeming creed of Christ.**

Brontë would have been very familiar with these 'narrow human doctrines'. Her father was a broad-minded and tolerant man with an optimistic and cheerful view of religion. He adhered to the non-conformist evangelical wing of the Anglican Church, which was, in its early days, responsible for the reform of a number of social abuses, such as the abolition of the slave trade. However, the children's aunt was a strict Calvinist believing in predestination and damnation, and so, even at the family dinner table, there would have been lively discussions.

The debates would have included:

- The challenge to faith posed by new scientific discoveries.
- The problems posed by a more historical approach to biblical criticism.
- Whether God's omnipotent power and knowledge meant that he had already, before the Creation, predestined the salvation of individuals, leading to an elect few who are saved, or whether Christ died for all and so everyone is capable of being born again.
- Whether God had no direct involvement with the individual destinies of human beings, or whether each individual can make direct contact with God through prayer.

Literary context

Fictional autobiography

In the seventeenth century, after the Restoration, authors such as Aphra Behn, John Bunyan and Daniel Defoe wrote books we can term 'proto-novels', which have a story rather than a plot, relating a sequence of events with little development in the central characters. It is not until the eighteenth century that true novels emerged. By this time, the form had been developed so that, instead of a series of events being narrated chronologically, writers constructed a plot that linked events together, exploring cause and effect, revealing significances and reaching a planned conclusion.

The genre grew in popularity with the expansion of the middle class, because the daughters of tradesmen were better educated than their parents, but they were not permitted to work or study for a career. Like the wives and daughters of the landed gentry and the professional class, they had servants to do most of the housework, so they had plenty of leisure time. Circulating libraries started up to make it possible for people to read more books than they could afford to buy, so there was a great demand for entertaining fiction.

Memoir-novels

At the beginning of the eighteenth century, there emerged a new form of novel, fictional autobiography or 'memoir-novels'. The first well-known memoir-novel is *Robinson Crusoe*, which was published in 1719. Crusoe relates his fall from grace as he defies his parents and runs away to sea, then the bulk of the novel traces his slow, painful, redemptive journey back to a state of grace. He is an educated man from a 'good family', and so he narrates his experiences and achievements meticulously, because he is recording the nature of his moral survival and redemption.

Seven years later, Jonathan Swift published the more complex *Gulliver's Travels*, for which he created another very reliable narrator. As a surgeon, Lemuel Gulliver is well educated and informed, not only professionally but also politically. His travels take him to extraordinary and fantastic societies, which he observes closely, and the details of his experiences he records scrupulously, as is expected from a medical practitioner. However, as his name implies, he is easily 'gulled' and seems oblivious to the parallels with his own society that Swift's satire is intended to ridicule.

Epistolary novels

It is not until Samuel Richardson, in the 1740s, that novels with first-person narratives achieved the moral introspection and psychological insight that characterises *Jane Eyre*. In his 'epistolary' novel, *Clarissa*, Richardson weaves together four main narrative voices, supported by various minor characters of differing age, class, and point of view, to construct a novel of great psychological complexity.

Context

Aphra Behn (1640–1689) was a prolific Restoration dramatist and one of England's first professional female writers, and her use of the narrator's voice makes her writing unique for its time.

Context

Daniel Defoe (c. 1660–1731) was an English writer and journalist. As the author of *Robinson Crusoe*, Defoe helped to popularise the novel as a form in Britain.

Context

Samuel Richardson (1689–1761) was an eighteenth-century English writer and printer known for writing three epistolary novels.

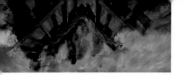

Romanticism

When people say that Brontë was influenced by Romantic writers, they are not referring to the fact that *Jane Eyre* is a love story about a Cinderella figure who eventually marries the man she adores. The Romantic period refers to a movement in the arts and ways of thinking that pervaded Europe at the end of the eighteenth century and the beginning of the nineteenth. Many writers, artists and musicians reacted against the neo-classical Age of Reason that characterised eighteenth-century thought. Instead of prizing reason and logical thinking, the new thinkers insisted that the emotional side of human responses was more important, that the brain should learn from the heart and from natural instinct, that the imagination held purer truths than the mind. Nature was all important, and some writers even rejected established religion and worshipped nature instead. In place of the eighteenth-century fascination with all things classical, writers and painters turned to the medieval, the Gothic, the foreign, the exotic, and the supernatural.

Reason versus nature

Brontë read widely among the Romantics, and it is easy to see their influence in *Jane Eyre*. Jane values reason, and indeed it dictates her behaviour when she leaves Thornfield, but love is more important to her. When she has to choose between a man she admires and the man she loves, she realises she needs love more than intellectual challenges. After meeting Eliza and Georgiana again, Jane concludes 'Feeling without judgment is a washy draught indeed; but judgment untempered by feeling is too bitter' (p. 272).

Jane is strongly influenced by nature, and looks there first for protection and guidance. After leaving Thornfield, she finds somewhere sheltered to sleep and some berries to eat, and only then does she say her 'evening prayers', as if by routine rather than need. Not until nightfall does she feel 'the might and strength of God' (p. 373). For Jane, nature has a personality; she has human moods and moral impulses. She is consoling, guiding and morally uplifting. There is a suggestion that Jane is tempted to worship nature, seeing the necessity to conceal her feelings for Rochester as 'Blasphemy against nature' (p. 204).

Top ten *quotation* ❯

For the Romantics, inspired moments cannot be summoned at will; they come unbidden, but the presence of nature is important. It is significant that the room is full of moonlight when Jane hears Rochester's voice. She runs into the garden and declares that 'it is the work of nature' (p. 483).

Marriage

Brontë embraces the Romantics' style of writing, but not their values. Although Romantics believed that their writing should be morally uplifting, many of them condoned illicit love, whereas Jane thinks rationally that, if she gave in to Rochester and became another of his mistresses 'he would one day regard me with the same feeling which now in his mind desecrated their memory' (p. 359). Jane does not live for the moment nor succumb to her feelings; she overcomes them and is rewarded. Jane trusts in God and her own self-respect. Brontë respects the institution of marriage, even as she recognises its drawbacks. If Jane had married St John, she would have lost her precious independence.

Brontë embraces the Romantics' style of writing, but not their values

Social reform

This emphasis on the importance of the individual is to be found in all Romantic writers. Inspired by the revolution in America with its Declaration of Human Rights, the French revolutionary cry of 'Liberty, Equality, Fraternity', and by the abolition of the slave trade, people began to argue for reform in England. Romantic thinkers argued not just for freedom for themselves but also for reforms in society, asserting that every individual has the same rights; the established social and political structures need to change to uphold these rights. Although Brontë graphically describes the lives of governesses, and the hardships faced by children in charity schools, she does not advocate reform. Nevertheless, she does expose hypocrisy in Mr Brocklehurst and strongly demonstrates that religion should not support the social structures that oppress ordinary people.

> **Context**
>
> The Slave Trade Act of 1807 abolished the slave trade in the British Empire, but not slavery itself, which remained legal until the Slavery Abolition Act 1833.

Rosamond Oliver is the one character in the book who is a social reformer, bringing education to the village children, not only boys but also girls. She, however, is dismissed by Jane as a 'sweet girl — rather thoughtless' (p. 430). It seems ironic to a twenty-first-century reader that Jane, who thinks only of herself, despising the 'heavy-looking, gaping rustics' (p. 422) she has to teach, is so dismissive of the young woman who actively embraces social reform, spending much of her allowance on tackling their ignorance and sharing some of the teaching herself. When married, Jane apparently does nothing for anyone other than her immediate family, applauding herself for finding a more indulgent school for Adèle.

Exotic imagery

The Romantics used imagery, usually natural or exotic, as a way of suggesting ideas rather than stating them directly. A good example is explored in the first extended commentary in the *Working with the text* section on pp. 87–89 of this guide.

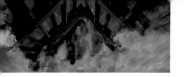

It is the fact that
Rochester is
already married,
rather than his
wife's madness,
that is essential
for the plot

It is the fact that Rochester is already married, rather than his wife's madness, that is essential for the plot. However, this device allows Brontë to introduce many Romantic elements. Thornfield is battlemented, like a medieval castle. Bertha herself is described as a monster or demon. She comes from the West Indies, an exotic place where English reserve and decorum may not be so valued. To escape her, Rochester has travelled widely in Europe and has had a succession of foreign mistresses. In the midst of all this Gothic horror and foreignness, the central figure of Jane seems to embody English reserve, self-restraint and Quakerish plainness.

The creative impulse

Romantics believed that the human mind is a complex and profound entity: a living, changing, mysterious organism whose most valuable powers are its imagination and creativity. The irrational and unknowable parts of the subconscious human mind are the source of the artistic drive; so Jane saw her paintings with her 'spiritual eye' before she attempted to embody them. Writers and artists have visions and aspirations beyond those of ordinary people but they are unable to express themselves fully in their writing or art, and are 'tormented' like Jane at 'the contrast between my idea and my handiwork' (p. 148).

To the Romantic, a human being is an immortal spirit trapped within a mortal frame, and so a writer can never be completely at home in the physical universe but will be continually aspiring after eternity, and this explains Jane's ecstasy at St John's proposal: 'Religion called — Angels beckoned — God commanded — life rolled together like a scroll — death's gates opening, showed eternity beyond' (p. 482). Ultimately, human experience is too complex and profound to be fully understood, and the soul is all important, so, after she hears Rochester's voice, she feels that 'the doors of the soul's cell' had been opened; 'it had wakened it out of its sleep' (p. 486).

Brontë's reading of Romantic poets and novelists has strongly influenced her style, but not her thinking. She remains the daughter of a parson, entirely caught up with her family and her own frustrations as a woman in a man's world. *Jane Eyre* is a strongly religious book, influenced as much by *The Pilgrim's Progress* as by the Romantics.

The Pilgrim's Progress

Brontë makes several references to this allegorical novel written by John Bunyan in the seventeenth century. Bunyan tells, through the device of a dream, how his hero, Christian, travels from the City of Destruction to the Celestial City.

In her references to Bunyan's work, Brontë invites her readers to read *Jane Eyre*, on one level, as a mythic quest. Jane struggles from the imprisonment of her childhood towards independence and equality. Like all women in a patriarchal society, she must meet and overcome oppression at Gateshead, humiliation at Lowood, temptation of the flesh at Thornfield and temptation of the spirit at Marsh End. Instead of making her story overtly allegorical, like Bunyan, Brontë adopts the form of a *Bildungsroman*, a term that refers to a novel that is an account of the youthful development of a hero or heroine, using a realistic framework to describe the various ups and downs from which the character achieves self-knowledge.

It is, however, worth noting the echoes of, and direct references to, *The Pilgrim's Progress*. After her furious outburst at Mrs Reed, Jane stands in the garden, whispering the words of Bunyan's Christian over and over again: 'What shall I do?' Later, when she saves Rochester from the fire, she is unable to sleep, and in her agitation she says 'I thought sometimes I saw beyond its wild waters a shore, sweet as the hills of Beulah' (p. 177).

After her hopes of marriage are shattered, Brontë uses an allegorical technique as Jane personifies elements of her personality. 'Conscience' told 'Passion' that 'she had yet but dipped her dainty foot in the slough, and swore that with that arm of iron he would thrust her down to unsounded depths of agony' (p. 343). Unlike Christian, however, she meets no 'Help' to save her from the 'Slough of Despond', and she has to tear herself away. Alone on the moor, she reflects on her situation, accepting that, 'The burden must be carried' (p. 374). It was 'the burden that was upon his back' that prevented Christian from extricating himself from the Slough, but the burden fell away when he saw the cross and the sepulchre. Significantly, Jane hears a church bell, but she does not go into the church. The Celestial City is the goal of those who accept the Church's teaching that we suffer in this life but will gain our reward in the next; it is not Jane's goal.

Jane swoons at Marsh End, just as Mercy swooned outside the Wicket gate after struggling across the Slough of Despond. Jane was lifted up by St John just as Mercy was lifted up by the keeper of the gate. Finally, at the end of Jane's journey, she has won through to Beulah and a life that is 'supremely blest', but she has rejected St John's certainty of an eternity in heaven. Brontë reminds us again of *The Pilgrim's Progress* at the very end of the novel, when St John faces death eagerly, anticipating 'his

Context

Christian's journey is beset by troubles, represented by images including the Slough of Despond, Castle of Giant Despair, and Valley of the Shadow of Death. Christian meets helpful and destructive characters, with appropriate names, e.g. Evangelist, Mr Worldly Wiseman, Mr Legality and his son, Civility.

Context

'Beulah' is derived from the Hebrew word for 'married'. Bunyan tells his readers that, in the Land of Beulah, 'the sun shineth night and day'.

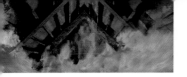

sure reward, his incorruptible crown' (p. 521). He has devoted his life to guiding others to the Celestial City, like the warrior Great-heart, 'who guards his pilgrim convoy from the onslaughts of Apollyon'.

Gothic fiction

Writers have always exploited the way in which readers or theatre-goers enjoy the thrill of being scared. *Beowulf* would not have delighted listeners and readers for more than a millennium, if the composer had not introduced terrifying monsters to threaten the harmony of the mead-hall. In the middle of the eighteenth century, Horace Walpole initiated a craze for these thrills in novels. He called his book: *The Castle of Otranto: A Gothic Story*.

Gothic fiction, in whatever medium, works by introducing the unfamiliar, the inexplicable, the irrational into a familiar, safe and realistic world. They are tales of mystery and fear, designed to chill the spine and curdle the blood, but only enough to evoke a delightful horror.

The earliest stories featured a beautiful young woman who would be abducted and threatened with seduction, or worse. The plot would move from the secure comfort of the parental home to the menacing environment of the abductor's abode. This would typically be an isolated, medieval castle with locked doors, dark corners and mysterious happenings. The helpless heroine would eventually be saved by the handsome, safe, young man who loves her. Many Gothic novels were written by women and they have been seen to represent a young woman's fear of marriage. In the eighteenth century, marriage for the educated, novel-reading class was often a business arrangement. Even if the young woman was lucky enough to marry for love, she would be chaperoned throughout the courtship and so have no opportunity to get to know her husband before the wedding. Her apprehension about married life and her future spouse was therefore quite understandable.

Sophisticated Gothic

By the nineteenth century, the appeal of the conventional Gothic horror novel was beginning to wane and novelists were using its stock ingredients in more sophisticated ways. Brontë blends its elements with a realism that gently mocks the overactive imagination of her heroine. Jane compares the corridor of the third storey of Thornfield with Bluebeard's castle, evoking Charles Perrault's fairy tale in which Bluebeard's young wife finds the corpses of his previous wives hanging on the walls of a locked room. However, 'The foul German spectre — the vampire'

Context

The Goths were an ancient Germanic tribe from the so-called 'Dark Ages', which lost its ethnic identity in the sixth century.

Context

Horace Walpole (1717–97), an English art historian and politician, is now remembered mainly for Strawberry Hill, his home in London, where he revived the Gothic style of architecture, and for his Gothic novel, *The Castle of Otranto*.

Context

Mrs Ann Radcliffe (1764–1823) helped to popularise the Gothic novel, as well as make it socially acceptable. She made sure that any seemingly supernatural events in her novels were explained by natural causes, and that her heroines' conduct was impeccable.

(p. 327), who tears Jane's veil is, in reality, his unhappy first wife. Rochester is no murderer and, in fact, it was not unknown for a woman to be locked up if her husband decided she was mad.

When Jane hears Rochester's horse approaching, she thinks of the Gytrash, 'a North of England spirit' which 'sometimes came upon belated travellers' (p. 132). The huge dog that appears out of the gloom appears 'exactly one mask of Bessie's Gytrash — a lion-like creature with long hair and a huge head'. Brontë, however, undermines Jane's fanciful imaginings with humour. The 'Gytrash' is Pilot, a friendly dog who wags his tail at Jane; the Byronic hero, far from being 'mad, bad, and dangerous to know', falls from his horse and needs Jane's help to remount. When his bed is set on fire to the accompaniment of a 'demoniac laugh' and 'goblin-laughter', Brontë dispels the Gothic atmosphere as Rochester wakes cursing, 'fulminating strange anathemas at finding himself lying in a pool of water' (p. 174).

Unlike the conventional heroine, Jane is neither beautiful nor a helpless victim. Although, in appearance, Rochester is a typical Gothic hero, he is vulnerable; he has a strong feeling of responsibility for Adèle and for his first wife, and he was reluctant to commit bigamy, preparing to do it only because he had become convinced that Jane would refuse to live with him as his mistress.

Brontë deviates from the conventional Gothic novel again in her presentation of St John. At first, he appears to be the young, handsome and devout hero who saves the heroine, but we eventually realise that he is more dangerous than Rochester. Brontë has drawn out his piety to a threatening extreme so that Jane declares, 'If I were to marry you, you would kill me. You are killing me now' (p. 475). This appears a melodramatic accusation, but Jane reflects the prejudice of her time in believing that she would die if she went to India.

The supernatural

Gothic fiction was designed to intensify the reader's emotional response by bringing elements of horror into a romantic novel. Brontë combines Gothic elements with a rational realism. The supernatural references are mostly metaphorical and, when she does introduce supernatural elements, like the white human form who advises her to 'flee temptation', it is usually in a dream.

The one event that is difficult to explain is the moment of telepathy when Jane and Rochester hear each other's voices. Jane, however, tries to explain it rationally, rejecting superstition and comparing the sensation with an electric shock, as if it is, in reality, the moment when she

> **Context**
>
> William Thackeray had his wife confined to an asylum for the insane in 1840 because she suffered from post-natal depression after the birth of their third daughter.

Top ten *quotation* 〉

realises 'It was *my* time to assume ascendancy. *My* powers were in play and in force' (p. 484). For Rochester, hearing Jane's voice appears to be his reward for eventually turning to God. Although Brontë does use a supernatural event, she does so to reinforce her main themes rather than contribute to the horror.

Satire

Satire is a protest, a way of expressing anger and indignation by ridiculing and bringing scorn upon its targets.

We have seen how Brontë combined humour with the Gothic tradition, but she also uses humour to load contempt upon the kinds of people she despises.

The Brocklehursts

As a child, Jane compares Mr Brocklehurst with the wolf in *Red-Riding Hood*, but the mature narrator mocks his rigidity with the description: 'bending from the perpendicular, he installed his person in the arm-chair' (p. 39).

Who can take Mr Brocklehurst seriously when, after his pious lecture against vanity and the lusts of the flesh, his wife and daughters enter? With well-targeted humour, Jane notes 'They ought to have come a little sooner to have heard his lecture on dress.' Not only are they 'splendidly attired in velvet, silk, and furs', but their hair is elaborately curled and Mrs Brocklehurst even 'wore a false front of French curls' (pp. 76–77).

Rochester's house guests

Brontë's description of Rochester's visitors attacks arrogance and pomposity; she draws pen-caricatures that undermine their pretensions. 'The ladies Lynn and Ingram', for instance, 'nodded their two turbans at each other, and held up their four hands in confronting gestures of surprise, or mystery, or horror…like a pair of magnified puppets', a simile that neatly punctures their 'solemn conferences' (p. 218).

When Mason is attacked, and the night is disturbed by his blood-curdling scream, the Gothic horror of the mysterious attack is effectively juxtaposed with the humour in the image she creates. The guests 'ran to and fro; they crowded together: some sobbed, some stumbled: the confusion was inextricable' (p. 239). Even the colonel is bemoaning that he cannot find Rochester. When the latter appears, he is almost strangled by the clinging Misses Eshton, 'and the two dowagers, in vast

Context

Brontë dedicated *Jane Eyre* to the satirist William Makepeace Thackeray, saying: 'I regard him as the first social regenerator of the day, as the very master of that working corps who would restore to rectitude the warped system of things.'

white wrappers, were bearing down on him like ships in full sail'. This exaggerated simile conjures up an amusing cartoon image of the poor man being throttled on one side and about to be engulfed by the older women's voluminous night attire.

Eliza Reed

Jane's satirical comment on her cousin's decision to enter a convent is 'The vocation will fit you to a hair… much good may it do you' (p. 279). This says a lot about Brontë's attitude to Roman Catholicism.

Critical context

Contemporary criticism

The novel, published under the pseudonym Currer Bell, was immediately popular, praised for its vigour and boldness, its freshness and originality, its powers of thought and expression. However, it also proved controversial. Some reviewers complained about the improbable plot and the suggestions of supernatural intervention; some were outraged by the manner in which the young Jane confronted adults, and the grown woman confronted the supposedly superior sex; some accused the writer of attacking religion in the characterisation of the hypocritical Mr Brocklehurst.

Later, when it was known to have been written by a woman, it still sold extremely well but attracted criticism from both conservatives and radical feminists. Conservatives regarded it as politically subversive. Brontë challenged the contemporary perception of women by portraying Jane as intelligent and passionate, equal to men in her capacity for intellectual aspiration as well as the depth of her sexual desire and the force of her anger. Many readers felt that God had made Jane a penniless orphan, and she ought to be grateful for the charity offered by her benefactors instead of expecting equality.

An autobiographical narrative necessarily asserts the importance of the individual, and invites that individual to express indignation at society's treatment of her. In both her writing and her paintings, Jane asserts her individuality. Politically this was subversive because, if each individual is valuable in his, or her, own right, then each individual should have the right to vote. Britain, however, was not a democracy; only male landowners were permitted to vote.

> **Context**
>
> 'It is one of the most powerful domestic romances which has been published for many years' (*The Atlas*).
>
> 'It is a book of decided power…the object and the moral of the work is excellent' (*The Examiner*).
>
> 'We do not hesitate to say that the tone of mind and thought which has overthrown authority and violated every code, human and divine, abroad, and fostered Chartism and rebellion at home, is the same which has written *Jane Eyre*' (Elizabeth Rigby, *Quarterly Review*, 1848).

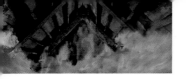

However, outspoken though she is about social injustice, Brontë was also criticised by contemporary feminists. Her friend, Mary Taylor, complained that she was soft on the 'rights of woman' issue. Mary felt that equal opportunity to work was an important issue that should be addressed head on. For Brontë, sentiment was more important than rights. At the end of the novel, Brontë comes down firmly on the side of 'self-sacrificing love'. In response to an article on the emancipation of women by John Stuart Mill, Brontë wrote to Mrs Gaskell that 'if there be a natural unfitness in women for men's employment, there is no need to make laws on the subject; leave all careers open; let them try'. However she criticises him for ignoring the heart: 'I think the writer forgets there is such a thing as self-sacrificing love and disinherited devotion.'

Brontë was not a campaigning social reformer, like her friend Elizabeth Gaskell, but her novel does reflect issues and changes in her society. Jane expresses approval of Lowood once it is run compassionately, calling it a 'truly useful and noble institution' (p. 100), even though its education programme is still designed to prepare the daughters of impoverished gentry for a life of duty and service.

Context

John Stuart Mill (1806–73) was an influential nineteenth-century British classical liberal thinker. His works on liberty justified freedom of the individual in opposition to unlimited state control.

Modern criticism

Feminist criticism

Recent feminist critics attempt to describe and interpret women's experience as depicted in literature. They question the long-standing dominant male ideologies, patriarchal attitudes and male interpretations in literature. They challenge traditional and accepted male ideas about the nature of women and how women are supposed to feel, act and think. Feminist critics interpret *Jane Eyre* less for what Brontë advocates and more for her struggle against the cultural inhibitions she was conditioned by. Her female protagonist, for example, could not actually express her sexual desire, so Brontë had to employ imagery to suggest it.

Many of the unrealistic melodramatic elements of the novel are perceived by feminist critics as evidence of Brontë battling against the contemporary social mores and resorting to Gothic characters, events and imagery in order to suggest what she cannot express in words. Sandra Gilbert and Susan Gubar, in their widely acclaimed study of nineteenth-century women writers *The Madwoman in the Attic* (1979), read her forcefulness when she breaks away from St John after hearing Rochester's call as:

> ...the climax of all that has gone before...The plot device of the cry is merely a sign that the relationship for which

both lovers had longed is now possible, a sign that Jane's metaphoric speech of the first betrothal scene has been translated into reality : 'my spirit…addresses your spirit, just as if we both had passed through the grave, and we stood at God's feet, equal — as we are!' (p. 367)

Psychoanalytic criticism

Psychoanalytic critics see literature as like dreams. Both are fictions, inventions of the mind that, although based on reality, are, by definition, not literally true. The theory is that much of what lies in the unconscious mind has been repressed, or censored, by consciousness and emerges only in disguised forms, such as dreams, or in an art form, such as painting or writing. They interpret the author's purpose in writing as being to gratify secretly some forbidden wish that has been repressed into the unconscious mind. So the novel is seen as wish-fulfilment on the part of the author with its plain, poor, intelligent heroine falling madly in love with the equally passionate, masterful Byronic hero, but marrying him on equal terms rather than allowing herself to be dominated.

Some critics interpret the novel as Brontë's subconscious exploration of her relationship with her father. The male characters all try to dominate and control Jane and she submits to their authority until they try to make her do something that is against her nature. Diane Sadoff sees *Jane Eyre* as a novel that allowed Brontë to understand, master, and free herself from her relationship with her own father.

The novel is also perceived as an exploration of Jane's own repressed subconscious. Gilbert and Gubar suggest that Bertha is Jane's night-time double. Jane wants to be Rochester's equal; Bertha is his equal in size and strength. Jane does not like the 'vapoury veil'; Bertha tears it in two. Jane wants to put off 'the bridal day', which she dreads as well as longs for; Bertha delays the wedding. Jane dreams of Thornfield in ruins; Bertha destroys it. 'Bertha', they conclude, 'is Jane's truest and darkest double; she is the angry aspect of the orphan child, the ferocious secret self Jane has been trying to repress ever since her days at Gateshead.'

When she decides to leave Thornfield, her conscience tells her 'you shall tear yourself away, none shall help you: you shall yourself pluck out your right eye; yourself cut off your right hand' (p. 343). This strange prophecy comes true when she marries the crippled Rochester and becomes 'bone of his bone, and flesh of his flesh' (p. 519). It is as if her subconscious wish to be on an equal footing with Rochester maims him to make him dependent on her, removes the impediment to

Context
Sigmund Freud (1856–1939), the Jewish Austrian originator of psychoanalysis, is considered one of the most original and influential thinkers of the first half of the twentieth century. The term 'Freudian' refers to his belief that early childhood experience affects all adult responses to life through the workings of the subconscious, where repressed urges lurk and reveal themselves in dreams and through 'Freudian slips'.

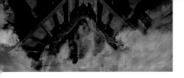

their marriage, and destroys Thornfield, where she had been his social inferior.

Marxist criticism

The Marxist perspective is that works of literature are conditioned by the economic and political forces of their social context. Not only is Brontë advocating the rights of the individual and universal education, but the whole plot of the novel is dictated by the need to create equality between a penniless orphan who arrives at Thornfield as a servant and her wealthy and dominant employer. She has to leave Thornfield and achieve independence; he has to become weaker and more dependent. Only when social conventions have been observed can they come together as equals and achieve a fulfilling and loving relationship.

In *Myths of Power,* Terry Eagleton reads Brontë's novels as 'myths which work towards a balance or fusion of blunt bourgeois rationality and flamboyant Romanticism, brash initiative and genteel cultivation, passionate rebellion and cautious conformity'. It is the tensions between these opposites that give *Jane Eyre* its dramatic power and lasting appeal.

Post-colonial criticism

Post-colonial critics oppose the view that 'culture' refers exclusively to 'high' culture and place a great deal of emphasis on the practice of everyday life. They focus on culture in relation to ideologies, which are different ways of viewing the world held by classes or individuals holding power in a given social group. Post-colonial critics have explored *Jane Eyre* in the context of the British Empire and the patronising attitudes of the dominant Christian English society to British colonies.

Bertha might have evoked British anxieties about having to deal with the other cultures under British dominion, and Bertha's imprisonment might signify Britain's attempts to control and contain the influences of these subject cultures. Rochester's marriage to Bertha represents the British Empire's cultural and economic exploitation of its colonial subjects; Edward Rochester's wealth was made on the backs of slaves in the West Indies. St John Rivers goes as a missionary to India, with arrogant hopes 'of carrying knowledge into the realms of ignorance — of substituting … religion for superstition', which is another way of exercising control (p. 431).

Elsie Michie, a post-colonial critic, explains: 'Colonial dominance was at once a civilising mission and a violent subjugating force.' Jane sees being a missionary as God's work; she anticipates 'noble cares and sublime results'. However, the extensive use of military imagery does suggest the 'violent subjugating force'. St John enlists her 'under His standard', and he prizes her 'as a soldier would a good weapon'; Jane speaks of his 'measured warrior march' and offers him 'a fellow-soldier's frankness' (Chapter XXXIV).

Deconstruction

To deconstruct a text is to show that it can have interpretations that are opposites and yet intertwined. Terry Eagleton points out the broad opposites that intertwine in the novel. Close inspection will reveal particular examples. Brontë, for instance, gives us the perspective of the child, Jane Eyre, so we learn how she felt at the time, as well as the interpretation of the adult, Jane Rochester, who is telling her story. Rochester thinks his marriage destroyed him, but the reader can see that it gave him financial independence and social position. Jane is a modern woman, intellectually ambitious, independent, passionate, but at the same time she is trapped in nineteenth-century thinking, and to us she appears intellectually as well as socially snobbish.

Jane is a modern woman, intellectually ambitious, independent, passionate, but at the same time she is trapped in nineteenth-century thinking

Working with the text

Meeting the Assessment Objectives

The four key English literature Assessment Objectives (AOs) describe the different skills you need to show in order to get a good grade. Regardless of what texts or what examination specification you are following, the AOs lie at the heart of your study of English literature at AS and A2; they let you know exactly what the examiners are looking for and provide a helpful framework for your literary studies.

The AOs are there to support rather than restrict you, so don't look at them as encouraging a tick-box approach or a mechanistic reductive way into the study of literature. Examination questions are written with the AOs in mind, so, if you answer them clearly and carefully, you should automatically hit the right targets. If you are devising your own questions for coursework, seek the help of your teacher to ensure that your essay title is carefully worded to liberate the required AOs so that you can do your best.

Although the AOs are common to all the exam boards, individual specifications vary enormously in the way they meet the requirements. The boards' websites provide useful information, including sections for students, past papers, sample papers and mark schemes.

- AQA: **www.aqa.org.uk**
- EDEXCEL: **www.edexcel.com**
- OCR: **www.ocr.org.uk**
- WJEC: **www.wjec.co.uk**

However, your knowledge and understanding of the text still lie at the heart of A-level study. While there may be an emphasis on the different ways *Jane Eyre* can be interpreted and on considering the novel in relation to different contexts, in the end the study of literature starts with, and comes back to, your engagement with the text itself.

Working with AO1

AO1: Articulate creative, informed and relevant responses to literary texts, using appropriate terminology and concepts, and coherent, accurate written expression.

AO1 focuses on literary and critical insight, organisation of material and clarity of written communication. Examiners are looking for accurate spelling and grammar, and clarity of thought and expression, so make your points succinctly. Aim for cohesion; guide your reader clearly through your line of argument. Think carefully about your introduction, because your opening paragraph not only sets the agenda for your response but should provide the reader with a strong first impression. Try to use 'appropriate terminology' but don't hide behind fancy critical terms or complicated language you don't fully understand. 'Feature-spotting' and merely listing literary terms is a classic banana skin all examiners are familiar with.

The examiner does not want to do the work for you, wading through a long quotation to find the words that support your point, so choose your references carefully. Try to incorporate brief quotations into your own sentences, weaving them in seamlessly to illustrate your points and develop your argument. The hallmarks of a well written essay, whether for coursework or in an exam, include a clear and coherent introduction that orientates the reader, a systematic and logical argument, aptly chosen and neatly embedded quotations, and a conclusion that consolidates your case.

Working with AO2

AO2: Demonstrate detailed critical understanding in analysing the ways in which structure, form and language shape meaning in literary texts.

In studying a long novel it is wise to begin with the larger elements of form and structure before considering language. The fact that Brontë chose to write an autobiographical novel, apparently written in retrospect, has a considerable influence on her choices of language.

In order to discuss language in detail you will need to quote from the text, but the mere act of quoting is not enough to meet AO2. What is important is what you do with the quotation — how you analyse it and how it illuminates your argument. Moreover, since you will often need to make points about larger generic and organisational features such

TASK 14

Practise writing in analytical sentences, comprising a brief quotation or close reference, a definition or description of the feature you intend to analyse, an explanation of how Brontë has used this feature, and an evaluation of why she chose to use it.

as settings and scenes, which are much too long to quote, being able to reference effectively is just as important as mastering the art of the embedded quotation.

Working with AO3

AO3 is a double Assessment Objective that asks you to 'explore connections and comparisons' between texts as well as showing your understanding of the views and interpretations of others.

AO3i: Explore connections and comparisons between different literary texts.

Your examination board may require you to compare and contrast one or more other texts with *Jane Eyre*, and you should try to find specific points of comparison, rather than merely generalising. You will usually find it easier to make connections between texts if you try to balance them as you write, although sometimes a core text is more heavily weighted than a supporting text. Remember that connections and comparisons are not only about finding similarities; differences are just as interesting. Above all, consider how the comparison illuminates each text. It is not just a matter of finding the relationships and connections but of analysing what they show. When writing comparatively, you should use words and constructions that will help you to link your texts, such as 'whereas', 'in contrast', 'by comparison', 'similarly'.

However, if this AO is assessed in single-text questions, you could explore the connections with another nineteenth-century novel or novella such as *The Yellow Wallpaper* by Charlotte Perkins Gilman.

If you are analysing how Brontë uses imagery to suggest Jane's sexual arousal in Chapter XXIII (see *Extended Commentaries*), you may draw contrasts with a modern novel such as Margaret Atwood's *The Handmaid's Tale*, which has a much more explicit scene in a garden.

AO3ii: Look at various possible different interpretations and use these to develop your own.

To access the second half of AO3 effectively you need to measure your own interpretation of a text against those of your teacher and other students. By all means refer to named critics and quote from them if it seems appropriate, but the examiners are most interested in your personal and creative response. If your teacher takes a particular critical line, be prepared to challenge and question it; examiners do not like to read a set of scripts that all say the same thing. Top candidates produce fresh personal responses rather than merely regurgitating the ideas of

Context

The Yellow Wallpaper is an autobiographical novel from the point of view of a wife imprisoned by her doctor husband so she can recuperate from what he calls a 'temporary nervous depression — a slight hysterical tendency'.

Context

The Handmaid's Tale is a feminist dystopian novel by Canadian author Margaret Atwood. Set in a totalitarian theocracy that has overthrown the US government, it examines women in subjugation.

others, however famous or insightful their interpretations may be. The fact that *Jane Eyre* is a subjective narrative from the point of view of one character means that there are plenty of opportunities to suggest different interpretations of events.

For instance, different readers respond in various ways to the end of this novel. Some think that Brontë compromises her principles when she maims and blinds Rochester and gives Jane an inheritance in order to establish the equality she has demanded throughout. However, it could be argued that they are now equal, not because Rochester is weaker and Jane richer, but because both have come to know themselves more fully. Jane has achieved autonomy, not in gaining an inheritance, but in learning how to balance the different sides of her character. What Jane has been searching for is a home, and, with Rochester, she says, 'I was at perfect ease, because I knew I suited him' (p. 504).

Some think that Brontë compromises her principles because Jane finds happiness only through marriage. However, Jane is not only passionate but also strongly religious, so it is only in marriage that she can be completely fulfilled. She may seem to have abandoned her intellectual aspirations but she has supposedly directed her talents into writing her autobiography.

Some think that Brontë should not have engineered a happy ending, but it was not her intention to write a tragedy. The novel is morally uplifting because it demonstrates that a woman does not have to compromise her principles to find happiness. Jane has refused to bend to class and gender prejudice; she has refused to allow herself to be pushed against her nature; and she has demonstrated that a woman's quest for love need not stifle her intellectual, spiritual and emotional independence.

Your interpretation will be convincing only if it is supported by clear reference to the text, and you will be able to evaluate other readers' ideas only if you test them against the evidence of the text itself. Worthwhile AO3 means more than quoting someone else's point of view and saying you agree, although it can be very helpful to use critical views if they push forward an argument of your own and you can offer relevant textual support. Look for other ways of reading the text, possibly from a Marxist, feminist, post-colonial or psychoanalytic point of view, which are more creative and original than merely copying out the ideas of just one person. Try to show an awareness of multiple readings and an understanding that the meaning of the text is dependent as much upon what the reader brings to it as what the writer left there. Using modal verb phrases such as 'may be seen as' or 'could be represented as' implies that you are aware that different readers interpret texts in different ways at different

> The novel is morally uplifting because it demonstrates that a woman does not have to compromise her principles to find happiness

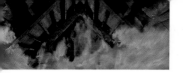

times. The key word here is plurality: there is no single meaning, no right answer, and you need to evaluate a range of other ways of making textual meanings as you work towards your own.

Working with AO4

AO4: Demonstrate understanding of the significance and influence of the contexts in which literary texts are written and received.

AO4 might at first seem less deeply rooted in the text itself but in fact you are considering and evaluating here the relationship between the text and its contexts. Note the word 'received': this refers to the way interpretation can be influenced by the specific contexts within which the reader is operating; for *Jane Eyre*, there is an immense gulf between its original contemporary context of production and the twenty-first-century context in which you receive it.

To access AO4 successfully you need to think about how contexts of production, reception, literature, culture, biography, geography, society, history, genre and intertextuality can affect texts. Place the text at the heart of the web of contextual factors that you feel have had the most impact upon it.

Examiners want to see a sense of contextual alertness woven seamlessly into the fabric of your essay rather than a clumsy bolted-on rehash of a website or your old history notes. Try to convey your awareness of the fact that literary works contain embedded and encoded representations of the cultural, moral, religious, racial and political values of the society from which they emerged, and that over time attitudes and ideas change until the views they reflect are no longer widely shared. There must be an overlap between a focus on interpretations (AO3) and a focus on contexts, so don't worry about pigeonholing the AOs here.

Context

Some awareness of the effect of the Industrial Revolution on society is essential here. The legal and economic position of women in Victorian society was markedly different from today, as were society's expectations of how a woman should behave. Religion was a strong influence on society, and Brontë draws on religious debates in her characterisation. The most significant literary influences on Brontë's writing are *The Pilgrim's Progress* and the Romantics.

Extract-based essay questions

Here are the questions to address when analysing any given extract from this novel:

- Why has Brontë included this passage? What is its importance?
- How does this passage fit into the narrative structure of the novel?
- Which of the themes is Brontë evoking here, and how does this passage fit into her treatment of that theme in the whole novel?
- What previous scenes do we need to recall in order to understand the implications of this passage?
- Does this extract foreshadow any future scenes?

- How reliable is Jane's account at this point?
- Is there any evidence that Jane is self-consciously crafting her narrative?
- Is there any evidence that Jane's narrative is enhanced by her imagination?
- What does this passage reveal about Jane's character, her feelings and thoughts?
- Does Brontë use any recurring images or symbols in this passage? If so, analyse how they fit into the overall pattern.
- If there is description, what mood is Brontë evoking and how does she do it?
- Is there any speech in this passage? If so, what does it add to the effectiveness, and what does it tell us about the speaker?
- Are there any words, phrases or metaphors that would reward close analysis?

Whole-text questions

Make sure you know which Assessment Objectives are examined by your board and concentrate on those. AO1 is assessed by looking at your whole essay and judging whether your writing skills and vocabulary are appropriate for A-level, whether your essay has been carefully planned and whether you are clearly very familiar with the whole text. You can prepare for the other Assessment Objectives.

Sample question: 'Jane Rochester brings a mature balance to her narrative.' How far and in what ways do you agree with this comment on the narrative method of Jane Eyre?

Possible approach

- If the board asks 'How far do you agree?' they expect you to agree to a certain extent and then disagree. This will give your essay a satisfying structure. For this question you need to analyse Brontë's use of a retrospective narrator and how the novel is structured. An overview of the narrative technique makes a good introduction to your essay, and this leads satisfyingly to close, detailed analysis of characterisation and language in the middle of your essay.
- You could argue that, at Gateshead and Lowood, the mature narrator helps the reader to understand feelings and thoughts that the child cannot articulate. However, once she falls in love with Rochester, Jane's narrative becomes unreliable as she wishes to present him positively.

> ### TASK 15
>
> How would you approach the following question?
>
> 'Relatives should be respected and loved, yet in literature they are often cruel and evil.'
>
> Using *Jane Eyre* pp. 19–20 as your starting point, from 'I was a discord in Gateshead Hall' to 'and to see an uncongenial alien permanently intruded on her own family group', explore the presentation of relatives.
>
> In your response, you should focus on Jane Eyre to establish your argument and you should refer to the second text you have read to support and develop your line of argument.

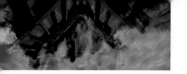

- An alternative line of argument might be that she does offer a mature balance in assessing her feelings and motives as a child and a young woman, but her language choices reveal that she still feels strong emotions, and Brontë's own prejudices sometimes seem to intrude.

- As evidence you could demonstrate how Brontë's experiences as governess have coloured Jane's attitude to children, both Adèle and her pupils at Morton, as well as to middle-class mothers. In Chapter XII, she comments on the cool language with which she describes Adèle, explaining 'I am not writing to flatter parental egotism, to echo cant, or prop up humbug; I am merely telling the truth.' This apparently balanced judgement reveals deep prejudice against the Victorians' idealisation of middle- and upper-class children in her use of strong colloquial language and harsh plosive consonants.

- At the end of Chapter XXVII, Jane Rochester's language makes clear that, even at the time of writing, she still feels guilty for doing the right thing and leaving Rochester. He has made her feel that she was 'the instrument of evil', an emotionally charged metaphor.

- Occasionally, Brontë makes Jane Rochester use the present and future tenses, as in Chapter XXXI when she writes of feeling degraded by becoming a village schoolteacher. Usually, however, Brontë uses the past tense, even when she implies immediacy with the adverb 'now' as in Chapter XXXV when Jane is comparing her resistance to St John with her resistance to Rochester: 'To have yielded then would have been an error of principle: to have yielded now would have been an error of judgement.'

- In the last third of your essay you should make insightful comparisons with additional appropriate texts, such as other nineteenth-century novels, or other fictional autobiographies.

- For AO4, you need to offer informed insight into the importance of such contextual issues as nineteenth-century attitudes to gender roles and social class, as well as Brontë's own experiences and views.

- See Sample essay 2 online at **www.philipallan.co.uk/literatureguidesonline** for a full answer to this question

Comparative questions

The examiners may expect you to offer a balanced essay with equal consideration given to each text, in which case you should compare and contrast them seamlessly throughout your essay. Alternatively, *Jane Eyre* may be your core text to be compared with a supporting text, in which case you should spend about two-thirds of your essay on Brontë's novel.

Student essay written under exam conditions

'Characters faced with difficult choices are the most interesting to read about.'

Explore the methods which writers use to present characters faced with difficult choices. In your response, you should focus on *Jane Eyre* to establish your argument and you should refer to the second text you have read to support and develop your line of argument.

Brontë wrote Jane Eyre as a first-person narrative. This means that when the protagonist and narrator, Jane, makes a decision, the reader is involved in her thought processes, capturing the reader's interest. Also, the narrative style means that, when decisions are made by other characters in the book, the reader is first introduced to Jane's opinions about their decision. Jane is a very biased narrator and influences the reader's judgement about other characters.

The introduction grasps the nettle from the start and gains marks for analysis of form and structure.

The choices made by characters in the book fall into two categories. People have to decide between following the heart or the mind, or, alternatively, choose between what is morally right and what is easy. These kinds of choices make the reader interested, as they are the decisions every individual must make in real life. This means that they can relate to what the characters experience and therefore sympathise with them. This therefore makes them more engaged in the novel.

One poignant example of an important and difficult choice made in *Jane Eyre* is when Jane decides to leave Thornfield. This decision demonstrates both the conflict of thought and emotion and also the conflict of what is easy. This is demonstrated when she says 'Conscience, turned tyrant, held Passion by the throat'. The personification of Conscience and Passion, enhanced by the use of capital letters, demonstrates how real these two antagonists are inside her, and it makes the reader visualise a physical battle between them. This visual technique is also effective in maintaining the reader's interest.

Good example of a sentence analysing both language and form.

The use of the derogatory noun 'tyrant' indicates that her conscience is strong and powerful, but the negative connotations indicate that Jane does not want it to win because she would enjoy staying with Rochester. However, she says about Passion that 'she had yet but dipped her dainty foot in the slough'. The noun 'slough' is very dirty and unpleasant, suggesting that her relationship with Rochester is tainted and wrong, as he is married. However, she describes

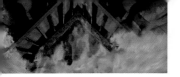

Passion's foot as 'dainty', which is a positive adjective, indicating that passion is not always wrong. This is further demonstrated by her choice of passion over logic when she comes back to Thornfield. Her use of gender is also significant as she makes the dominant figure 'Conscience' male and the weaker 'Passion' a woman. This suggests that the man in her life will always have dominance over her heart.

During this part of the book, she appears to have a conversation with herself, saying, "'Let another help me!' 'No; you shall tear yourself away'". This dialogue is written in the future tense as she narrates in the moment of her decision regarding what she was going to do. She even uses speech marks to show her inner conversation. This technique engages the reader as the internal dialogue is also a direct communication with the reader. It makes the reader visualise her torment as she experiences it, not as she looks back on it, having a greater impact on the reader's emotions. Her plea for help shows the difficulty she faces in her decision and that she is tempted by the wrong decision.

Carter, in *The Magic Toyshop*, shows the character of Finn making a difficult decision, and he is also tempted to take the wrong path. Finn had to decide whether or not to give in to his carnal desires when Uncle Phillip asked him to rehearse the play with Melanie. Even though Finn 'fancies' her, he chooses not to have sex with her as it is the morally right thing to do. His temptations were shown by his sudden burst of "'No,' Finn said aloud. 'No!'" This shows that he was about to do it when he forcefully stopped himself. Also he 'sprinted across the room, jumped into the cupboard and shut the door', which shows that he had to escape from Melanie to resist her. The verb 'sprinted' shows his urgency and his knowledge that he had to escape quickly before the damage was done. This is similar to when Jane was told to 'leave Thornfield at once' by her mind. The urgency of Finn contrasts with the slow speed of the build-up before 'Time began' again.

Though Finn's actions are quick, the reader is not yet involved in his thoughts so does not immediately understand why he acts the way he does. The situation is explained after the decision has been made, due to the narrative style. The omniscient narrator only narrates thoughts from Melanie's point of view, so Finn's thoughts are unknown until he explains to Melanie 'He [Uncle Phillip] wanted me to fuck you.' From the negative associations of the taboo word 'fuck', we see he had made the right decision. However, earlier on we are not sure as we only see Melanie's point of view and she is angry and sad that Finn left, saying that 'she felt cold and ill'.

Good example of analysis of form and structure.

Good link between the texts.

(NB: This essay is assessed only for AO1 and AO2)

Examiner's comment AO1: Secure knowledge of the texts underpins a clear line of argument. Reader guided confidently. Critical terminology used appropriately. However, the candidate did not leave time to pull the ideas together in a conclusion.

Examiner's comment AO2: Impressive close detailed analysis of language, structure and form.

Low grade A. A C-grade answer to this question is given online.

Transformational writing

Sample task

Write the letter St John might have written to Jane on the occasion of her marriage. You should aim to write in St John's voice, building upon Brontë's presentation of his character and capturing aspects of the writer's chosen form, structure and language.

Extract from answer

My dear Jane,

I cannot pretend that I am not disappointed by your choice, but I respect your decision. You have chosen earthly joys over Heavenly bliss, and I do hope that you will not be disappointed. I know you were of the opinion that I did not love you and valued you only for your capacity for work, but I am convinced we could have been happy. If I cared nothing for you, do you really think that I would have humiliated myself by asking for your hand a third time? True, you did not set my blood aflame like one other I could mention, but you are the woman I most wanted to accompany me through life. You will never know how much it hurt me to hear you accuse me of killing you, you whom I valued even above my own sisters.

I offered you the most glorious occupation man can undertake. Together we could have worked to the glory of God and towards an eternity in Heaven at our Maker's right hand, happy in the knowledge that we were helping to build His spiritual kingdom on earth. You could have shared my ambitions to bring light where there is darkness, freedom where there is slavery, faith where there is only superstition. You could have given your heart to God. Instead you have given it to a castaway, a weak and sinful man who is not worthy of this

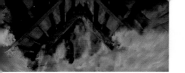

sacrifice. Perhaps you think now that saving his soul will be enough for you, but I know your character and your aspirations; you will not be happy merely as a wife and mother. Your spirit will chafe against the stagnation, and your intellect long for an enterprise in which you can challenge yourself and work to the greatest glory offered to one of God's humble servants.

Student's own commentary

In St John Rivers, Brontë has created a character who is uncompromising, so I think it will be very difficult for him to be sincerely happy for Jane, and the double negative in his first line demonstrates the difficulty he has writing a conventional letter. I also think Brontë strongly suggests that his feelings for Jane were stronger than he allowed himself to admit, and I have made him hint at this in a pained question.

St John is an eloquent preacher, used to impressing his congregation with polysyllabic, Latinate vocabulary, and will not be able to write a letter of congratulation without sermonising. I have tried to suggest his eloquent rhetoric with the triplet of parallel clauses in which he explains his ambitions. He uses many words and phrases from the semantic field of religion, including the symbolic use of darkness for ignorance, and he speaks in declaratives, confident that he has read Jane's character correctly. He uses the potential modal auxiliary verb 'could' to remind her what she has lost, and the future tense 'will' to predict how she will come to feel.

Examiner's comments: AO1 — quality of writing:

- Immaculate spelling, punctuation and grammar
- Vocabulary appropriate to a nineteenth-century clergyman
- Creative and original point of view (predicting that St John will not give up trying to influence Jane just because she is married)
- Creating and sustaining believable register
- Varied sentence structure which reflects source text

Examiner's comments: AO2 — form, structure and language:

- Sense that language used is a 'map of the character's mind'
- Sense that character chosen is understood, attitudes he displays are convincing and likely, based on close reading of text
- Figurative language
- Symbolism
- Specific reflections of Brontë's text which show seamless overarching understanding of text

Examiner's comments: AO3 — different interpretations:

- Fresh understanding of St John suggesting that his three proposals and the way he turned 'quite white' when she accused him of killing her indicated that he really did love her

Examiner's comments: AO4 — contexts:

- References/speech appropriate to era in which text is set
- Subtle references to the doctrine of Calvinists and their belief in election, predestination and reprobation

Further sample essays are provided online at **www.philipallan.co.uk/literatureguidesonline**

Extended commentaries

In all kinds of essay, you need to show that you can analyse form, structure and language in detail. Select key passages and practise analysing them, as well as setting them in the context of the whole novel, so that you have examples ready to include in your essays.

Two extended commentaries are given here; a third, on St John's proposal, pp. 462–65, can be found online.

1 Sunset in the orchard: pp. 286–88

Brontë introduces Chapter XXIII with a long description that sets the appropriate Romantic mood. The first three paragraphs offer a very visual portrayal of a dramatic sunset painted in words. Deep rich colours provide the backcloth for a solitary star, described metaphorically as a 'gem', sparkling and precious. This is typical of the way Romantic writers use nature to suggest deeply passionate feelings when it is not appropriate or acceptable to state them in the manner we have come to expect in the modern world. Jane's appreciation of the sunset's power and beauty suggests that she feels passionately and has a heart that responds to such Romantic moments.

As Jane enters the orchard, Brontë uses dramatic irony to evoke anticipation in the reader. Jane smells the 'well-known scent' of a cigar, and she realises that Rochester is standing at the slightly open library window and that she could be seen. She apparently thinks she turns aside into the orchard before Rochester sees her, but the reader

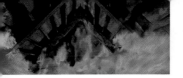

anticipates his following her. Through Jane's description, Brontë is able to suggest Jane's mood as she wanders in the orchard.

Jane describes the garden as 'Eden-like', a simile that suggests to the reader not only an innocent paradise but also the place where Eve was tempted. The orchard is separated from the house and garden by a high wall and a row of beeches, but only by a sunken fence from 'lonely fields'; this suggests closeness to nature and a separation from civilisation, a place where one can respond naturally to one's feelings without worrying about social conventions. The fragrance of the flowers is described as 'incense', suggesting a heady drug. Jane notices the early ripening cherries and gooseberries large as plums; this imagery carries a suggestion of fertility and has associations with the fruit of the Garden of Eden. The moth, which Rochester describes as 'so large and gay a night rover', is unusually 'great' and helps to give an exotic feel to the garden, supported by Rochester's comparison of it with insects in the West Indies. Another, essential, ingredient of a Romantic setting is 'the now-rising moon'.

Jane's description of the smell of the cigar as a 'fragrance', a 'scent' and a 'perfume' suggests that she finds it seductive rather than repellent. This could only be because of its association with Rochester, so the reader realises that she loves him before she admits it, even to herself. When Jane realises that Rochester is also in the orchard, Brontë changes from retrospective narrative in the past tense to a spontaneous present tense so that we can share Jane's feelings at the time. As the smell gets stronger she uses the strongest modal auxiliary verb to express the urgency in 'I must flee'. She does not explain why this governess needs to flee from her employer. He has not given her any indication that he is a threat, so presumably she is frightened of her own feelings.

Jane reverts to the past tense as she tells us what she remembers of her thoughts and describes her attempts to depart unnoticed. She still sounds surprised as she asks '— could his shadow feel?' The reader, however, is not surprised as Brontë has already suggested that he saw her from the library window. Perhaps Brontë wishes to suggest that Jane still cannot admit that, deep down, she hoped he would speak to her; this would have been impossibly precocious for a governess in Victorian times.

Jane admits that she did 'not like to walk at this hour alone with Mr Rochester in the shadowy orchard'. She perceives it as a 'fault' in herself that she cannot always frame an excuse quickly. As a governess, she knows she is expected to remain in the background and not act as if she is her employer's equal; however, she clearly wishes to stay and spend time with him and this is why she cannot make up a reason to depart. She seems torn between her feelings for him and what she perceives

PHILIP ALLAN LITERATURE GUIDE FOR A-LEVEL

as her duty. Clearly, at this point, because of the way in which her feelings have been heightened in the Romantic setting, she is unable to obey her reason, which tells her that there is no hope of marriage and any other liaison is quite out of the question. If she stays, however, she might give herself away, revealing her feelings to him, and make herself vulnerable. The 'evil' she speaks of cannot refer to Rochester, as he has done nothing untoward, so she must be speaking of her own feelings. She calls them 'evil' because her whole life she has been made aware that, as a woman, and as a dependant, she must not show her feelings. Whenever she has lost control of her emotions she has regretted it.

2 The conclusion

Jane is supposedly writing ten years after she arrived at Ferndean. It is interesting to analyse the language she uses to assess whether Brontë really wants us to believe that Jane has now found what she wanted and feels that she has made the right choices in her life.

Jane tells her readers, in superlatives, that she knows 'what it is to live entirely for and with what I love best on earth. I hold myself supremely blest' and that, when he was blind, Rochester loved her so truly, that 'he knew no reluctance in profiting by my attendance'. Three times she emphatically declares 'never did I weary' of doing things for him when he could not see. However, while he loved her 'truly', she loved him 'fondly'. Not only is she writing in the past tense when only ten years into their marriage, but 'fondly' sounds cooler than 'truly'. She says 'All my confidence is bestowed on him, all his confidence is devoted to me'; once again 'bestowed' sounds much cooler and more distant than 'devoted', as if her confidence is given as a gift. Her choice of language suggests that perhaps she does not love him quite as devotedly as he loves her.

On pp. 129–30, Brontë tells the reader that

> ...women feel just as men feel; they need exercise for their faculties, and a field for their efforts as much as their brothers do; they suffer from too rigid a restraint, too absolute a stagnation, precisely as men would suffer; and it is narrow-minded in their more privileged fellow-creatures to say that they ought to confine themselves to making puddings and knitting stockings, to playing on the piano and embroidering bags.

Jane is supposedly married when she writes this, which suggests that Brontë may not have been happy with the ending of this novel. Jane may

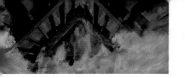

not feel as 'supremely blest' as she professes. Indeed, when they married, Jane wanted to become Adèle's governess once more, but 'my time and cares were now required by another — my husband needed them all'. Her time and cares are not freely given but 'required' by her husband, leaving her no opportunity to fulfil herself as a teacher. This woman who declared to Rochester on p. 293: 'I am no bird; and no net ensnares me; I am a free human being with an independent will' is now 'bone of his bone, and flesh of his flesh'. This metaphor suggests that not only her body but also her independence and individuality have been entirely taken over by her husband.

Brontë has chosen to end Jane's autobiography with a eulogy of St John Rivers. When Jane was asked by St John to go to India with him as a missionary, she considered that, as Rochester was lost to her, this occupation was 'truly the most glorious man can adopt or God assign' (p. 466). She wrote of its 'noble cares and sublime results', but, although tempted to go, she realised that he did not love her and 'if I join St John, I abandon half myself'. St John recognised that 'though you have a man's vigorous brain, you have a woman's heart' (p. 470); in the nineteenth century it was even more difficult than it is now for a woman to devote herself to both career and family. Jane chose love over intellectual fulfilment but, as she recognised, by doing so she abandoned the half of her that sought a vocation.

When she realises from his letters that St John is dying, she seems overwhelmed with admiration for the 'resolute, indefatigable pioneer'. He may be dying unnaturally young but, although she wept for this, his last letter 'filled my heart with divine joy'. Her adulation of him has not dimmed but she admits to no regrets. Jane has always had a strong will to live, unlike Helen Burns, and to have gone with him would have been to sacrifice not only half herself but her life also.

Top ten quotations

It is impossible to represent this complex novel in only ten quotations so I have selected those that illustrate the main theme of Jane's growth to maturity and her struggle to attain self-fulfilment.

1   **Something of vengeance I had tasted for the first time. As aromatic wine it seemed, on swallowing, warm and racy; its after-flavour, metallic and corroding, gave me a sensation as if I had been poisoned. (pp. 45–6)**

Jane explains how open rebellion against her aunt made her feel in a simile that compares the sensation to that of drinking aromatic wine. Just as wine feels 'warm and racy' as it is drunk, but leaves an unpleasant after-flavour, so the act of vengeance felt good while her temper was up but left her bitterly regretting the madness of her conduct.

> 'Yet it would be your duty to bear it, if you could not avoid it: it is weak and silly to say you *cannot bear* what it is your fate to be required to bear.' (p. 66)

2

It is from Helen Burns that Jane learns to endure those things that are beyond her control. Helen quotes Jane's own words and Brontë puts them in italics to suggest a contemptuous tone for a childish attitude.

> ...a tale my imagination created, and narrated continuously; quickened with all of incident, life, fire, feeling, that I desired and had not in my actual existence. (p. 129)

3

After three months at Thornfield, Jane admits to a restlessness that can be satisfied only in her imagination. By using a rhetorical triplet with the addition of a fourth item 'feeling', enhanced by the alliteration of /f/ and /l/, Brontë captures Jane's restlessness in her speech, suggesting that the mature Jane is reliving how she felt as an eighteen-year-old with an overdeveloped imagination.

> Did I forbid myself to think of him [Rochester] in any other light than as a paymaster? Blasphemy against nature! (pp. 203–4)

4

Although Jane is supposedly writing more than ten years after these events, Brontë dramatises her thoughts as a question and an exclamation, giving Jane's emotions an immediacy that invites the reader to share her feelings of outrage that her reason and duty have to deny nature, which she thinks of as a goddess, using 'blasphemy', an abstract noun from the semantic field of religion.

> 'Strong wind, earthquake-shock, and fire may pass by: but I shall follow the guiding of that still small voice which interprets the dictates of conscience.' (p. 233)

5

Brontë draws on a passage from the Bible when Rochester, disguised as a gypsy, correctly assesses Jane's character in her face. In I Kings 19:11–12, the prophet Elijah learns that the voice of the Lord is not in the strong wind, nor the earthquake, nor the fire, but in the still small voice that comes afterwards when he is alone. Rochester did not realise

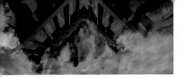

how true his prophecy was. When Jane's world is turned upside down as if there has been an earthquake, and her emotions are in turmoil, she follows her conscience and leaves Thornfield.

6

'Do you think, because I am poor, obscure, plain, and little, I am soulless and heartless? You think wrong! — I have as much soul as you — and full as much heart!' (p. 292)

As a child, Jane had told Mrs Reed, 'You think I have no feelings, and that I can do without one bit of love and kindness; but I cannot live so' (p. 44). With equal passion, Jane once again asserts her equal worth with other human beings. This time she uses more mature language with the abstract concepts of 'soul' and 'heart', the symbol of romantic love; however, she still feels that she is despised because of her poverty and physical appearance. Her sensitivity on these points comes out in the desperate list of four adjectives and the spontaneity of her outburst in the dashes that break up the speech. Whereas as a child she made a declaration, this time she questions, possibly not believing that Rochester could be so insensitive.

7

He [Rochester] stood between me and every thought of religion, as an eclipse intervenes between man and the broad sun. I could not, in those days, see God for His creature: of whom I had made an idol. (p. 316)

Just as, in an eclipse, the moon prevents people seeing the sun, so Jane's love for Rochester was so great that it stood between her and God. Brontë uses this image to show that Jane needed to stop making an 'idol' of the man, so that she could give God his rightful place. Jane has not completed her journey to maturity. She needs to learn to put human love in its proper place and not to lose sight of God in her worship of Rochester.

8

I was experiencing an ordeal: a hand of fiery iron grasped my vitals. Terrible moment: full of struggle, blackness, burning! Not a human being that ever lived could wish to be loved better than I was loved; and him who thus loved me I absolutely worshipped: and I must renounce love and idol. One drear word comprised my intolerable duty — 'Depart!' (p. 363)

When Rochester begs her to stay, Jane is torn between reason and feeling. She describes her dilemma in a metaphor that suggests intense physical pain. The fractured syntax of 'Terrible moment: full of struggle,

PHILIP ALLAN LITERATURE GUIDE **FOR A-LEVEL**

blackness, burning' suggests that Jane is reliving this pain as she writes and this is reinforced by the use of the present tense modal verb 'must'.

I will hold to the principles received by me when I was sane, and not mad — as I am now...They have a worth — so I have always believed; and if I cannot believe it now, it is because I am insane — quite insane: with my veins running fire, and my heart beating faster than I can count its throbs. (p. 365)

9

The future tense modal auxiliary verb 'will' and the present tense verb forms give the young Jane's determination not to give in to her feelings an immediacy to which the reader can relate as the mature woman relives this pivotal moment in her life. Significantly, she repeats the assertion that she is, at that moment, 'insane', inviting comparison with Bertha, a similarly passionate woman who seems not to have learned the principles to which Jane clings.

It was *my* time to assume ascendancy. *My* powers were in play and in force.' (p. 484)

10

Brontë employs a supernatural intervention to mark the point at which Jane realises that she is mistress of her own fate, emphasised by the italicisation of the first person singular determiner 'my'. She has been tempted to share the glory of St John's mission in India, but, when she asks heaven for guidance, she hears Rochester's voice. However, she balances passion with reason and prays before she returns to Thornfield.

Taking it further

Films

There are several films available, but they should be watched only after you have read the book as adapting a long novel for the screen always involves changes. The most recent are:

- The 1997 film, directed by Robert Young, starring Samantha Morton and Ciaran Hinds
- The 2006 film, made for the BBC and directed by Susanna White, starring Ruth Wilson and Toby Stephens
- A film is scheduled to be released in 2011, directed by Cary Fukanaga and starring Mia Wasikowska and Michael Fassbender

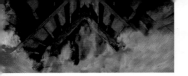

Books

Some useful books are:

- Barker, Juliet (1994) *The Brontës*, Weidenfeld and Nicolson
  - This is a very readable biography of the Brontë family, giving useful context and background information.
- Allott, Miriam (ed.) (1973) *Charlotte Brontë: Jane Eyre and Villette*, Macmillan Casebook Series
  - This collection of critical essays includes contemporary criticism as well as views from the mid-twentieth century.
- Newman, Beth (ed.) (1996) *Jane Eyre: Charlotte Brontë*, Bedford/St Martin's
  - This edition of the novel includes several studies in modern criticism.

Internet

Some useful websites are:

- **www.victorianweb.org** Click on 'Authors' and then 'Charlotte Brontë'
  A collection of links to extremely interesting essays and resources.
- **www.bronte.org.uk**
  The official website of the Brontë Society and museum, with details of their exhibitions and events.

For these and other weblinks go to **www.philipallan.co.uk/ literatureguidesonline**